Adaptive Business Continuity: A New Approach

A Rothstein Publishing Collection Book

David Lindstedt
Ph.D., PMP, CBCP

Mark Armour
CBCP

Kristen Noakes-Fry, ABCI, Editor

EPUB ISBN: 978-1-944480-40-0
PDF ISBN: 978-1-944480-41-7
PRINT ISBN: 978-1-944480-49-3

ROTHSTEIN PUBLISHING
A Division of Rothstein Associates Inc.

203.740.7400

info@rothstein.com
www.rothstein.com
Keep informed about Rothstein Publishing:

www.facebook.com/RothsteinPublishing
www.linkedin.com/company/rothsteinpublishing
www.twitter.com/rothsteinpub

i

EPUB ISBN: 978-1-944480-40-0
PDF ISBN: 978-1-944480-41-7
PRINT ISBN: 978-1-944480-49-3

Library of Congress Control Number: 2017952576

A Division of Rothstein Associates Inc.

203.740.7400

info@rothstein.com
www.rothstein.com
Keep informed about Rothstein Publishing:

www.facebook.com/RothsteinPublishing
www.linkedin.com/company/rothsteinpublishing
www.twitter.com/rothsteinpub

Dedication

To: Michael Carpenter and John Ellinger.

— David Lindstedt

To: Julie Armour and Philip Bigge.

— Mark Armour

Acknowledgments

While there are many people who helped influence our thinking on this subject, we want to acknowledge the initial members of the Adaptive Business Continuity think tank in particular:

- Philip Jones, Technology Resilience Manager, Sky Plc.
- Adele Johnston, Managing Director, AJ Continuity Consulting Ltd.
- Joe MacDonnell, Group Business Continuity Manager, Sky Plc.
- Sylvain Goyette, Director Strategic Development, Continuity Planning and Emergency Measures, Quebecor Media.
- Rod Crowder, Managing Director, OpsCentre.
- Dan Dorman, IT Service Continuity Program Manager, Alaska Airlines.
- Élaine Comeau, Senior Director, Business Continuity, Banque Nationale du Canada.
- Nina White, Business Continuity Consultant.

We also take this time to remember John Stagl for his thoughtfulness and encouragement.

Preface

Business Continuity Today

We believe we are at a turning point in the preparedness planning industry, specifically within the field of business continuity (BC).

Four primary drivers have led us to this conclusion:

1. Thought leaders have identified significant issues with many core practices of traditional continuity planning.
2. Many practitioners have found new and innovative ways to implement BC, creating successful practices beyond existing guidelines that have not yet coalesced into a single approach.
3. Organizations and executives are demanding more business value for their money, and return on investment (ROI) for BC and its practitioners is not always obvious.
4. Large-scale changes within related disciplines, such as project management and process improvement, along with the rapid growth of new global business methods, demand a more flexible and responsive approach to BC than many current practices provide.

Taking proper action in response to these drivers and capitalizing on the current situation will require those of us in the profession to look at BC and its practice in new ways. In this book, we present our alternative approach to traditional BC planning that aims to address these challenges and carefully shepherd a change in the discipline. We call this approach:

Adaptive Business Continuity

A large part of this book explains this new framework in detail. Before we can begin to outline this new approach, however, we must look at some practices that are likely to get in the way if not addressed. Therefore, Chapter 1 rightly starts with a critical examination of BC today before later chapters explain the Adaptive Business Continuity (Adaptive BC) approach.

How to Use this Book

We have organized the chapters of this book, by way of analogy, with the steps of rebuilding a house. After deciding how you want your new house to look, the first step is to identify and remove all the things that no longer properly belong in the kind of house you need. We have called Chapter 1 "Demolition," not because we are getting rid of the entire BC enterprise, but because there are certain BC activities and products that must be removed to provide the space we need to install something new. We then proceed through the rebuilding stages, namely foundation, framework, and finishing. Finally, we end with a chapter called "Dwelling," in which we consider what it might be like to live in this new home we have built.

While we believe that you will get the most value by reading the chapters in order, we have structured this book so that you can jump right in to whatever topic is most important to you. After the Introduction, which explores the original manifesto that helped drive the development of the Adaptive BC approach, the book is organized into five chapters:

- **Chapter 1: Demolition** – This chapter outlines the problems and shortcomings within traditional continuity planning. It explains why current practices in the BC discipline often do not produce the results that practitioners, participants, and leaders want. These chapters clear out ("demolish") a number of traditional practices that stand in the way of making needed improvements to the industry. Fixtures such as the business impact assessment (BIA), risk assessment (RA), and recovery time objective (RTO) can get us off on the wrong foot from the very beginning and need to be removed.

- **Chapter 2: Foundation** – This chapter provides a proper foundation for BC planning. To date, our profession has various collections of best and good practices; it does not have a reasoned theory upon which to build a discipline. This chapter provides, for the first time, an integrated theory of preparedness planning. This topic requires a more theoretical approach than other chapters in order to provide context for the planning activities that make up Adaptive BC.

- **Chapter 3: Framework** – This chapter introduces the specific approach for Adaptive BC. If you are looking for the practical nuts-and-bolts "how to" of the framework, this is the section for you. It outlines the individual steps, activities, and deliverables the practitioner creates in partnership with all levels of the organization.

- **Chapter 4: Finishing** – This chapter provides a narrative to help you envision what the Adaptive BC approach might look like in practice. It fleshes out the overall approach using specific examples in time and place. In these case studies, you will meet five fictitious practitioners as they implement the Adaptive BC approach in their organizations. Hopefully, these stories will inform and inspire you to take your next steps and get started right away within your own organization.

- **Chapter 5: Dwelling** – This chapter wraps up the book and offers a few thoughts on what the future of the BC industry might hold, including the promise of fun and innovation in your daily activities.

We are very pleased to offer this book to practitioners, leaders, and academics alike. We fully expect the BC profession to evolve and we look forward to playing a role in its continued development. It is our sincere hope that the ideas contained within this book will empower you and your efforts to further protect our organizations and communities.

David Lindstedt

Columbus, Ohio
April 2017

Mark Armour

Frisco, Texas
April 2017

Foreword

I was initially introduced to the work of David Lindstedt and Mark Armour through their Continuity 2.0 Manifesto. Fortunately, it was published at an opportune moment for me and for the profession. Like many practitioners, I was conscious of a growing feeling of disappointment and frustration with the largely monolithic approach of business continuity (BC) best practices. Put simply, traditional best practices no longer appeared to be a comfortable fit to the evolving needs of business today. For example, I saw how software packages that had once been the hallmark of a solid BC program were falling by the wayside, appearing to engender much activity but produce little value.

I was concerned that many organizations were moving away from the best practices that most of us had been taught, instead treating BC as "one and done" – doing just enough to remain compliant, checking and exercising the plan perhaps once a year, and considering that good enough.

In today's evolving business environment, the traditional approach is no longer anywhere near good enough! For, as complex risk specialist Warren Black notes, "...we are living in what is becoming known as the 'Agile Age,' an era that is driven by rapid, momentous and continuous change. The Agile World is one that is significantly more complex and unpredictable and it is a world whereby the ability to react and adapt quickly is critical to survival."

Clearly, the best practices of the BC profession have failed to adapt to this agile age in all its manifestations – from agile and lean methodologies to virtual or hierarchical organizational structures.

When I read the manifesto – the concepts of which are explained and expanded upon in this new book – I knew I had found my touchstone. I realized I had, for some time, been acting from these principles and beliefs. But I had also been feeling uneasy about deviating from many of the professional standards, opting instead to radically customize my practices to the culture and requirements of my organization. Now I could shed any residual guilt and step forward boldly to take further steps within my organization. In an atmosphere of experimentation, and as part of an effort to evolve the practice of my profession, I sought practical approaches to meeting the needs of an evolving business environment.

I regard this book and the practical concept of Adaptive BC as the next significant step in the evolution of our profession. It offers a firm theoretical base, meaningful and (finally!) useful metrics to track improvements, and it is brimming with immediately practical techniques for implementing this approach in any environment.

The Adaptive BC approach should feel familiar to anyone with exposure to the new agile practices, that is, repeating patterns of rapid, practical improvements. Agile practices feature simple but well defined value-driven objectives, easily aligned with organizational goals; frequent review and adaptation; and iterative development and improvement, where requirements and solutions evolve through collaboration between cross-functional teams.

In introducing you to this book, I would be remiss if I did not mention one of the most important elements of the Adaptive BC Approach – it's you, the practitioner! BC is a profession. The art of BC is expressed through using your experience, organizational knowledge, business acumen, and professional judgment to customize your approach in a way that complements the organizational values and culture, and addresses the stated organizational goals. Adaptive BC works best when you give yourself permission to exercise it… adaptively!

As David and Mark demonstrate in this book, the genius of Adaptive BC is that the measurement, communication, and demonstration of achieved objectives is not a separate annual or quarterly activity but is intrinsic to the ongoing process, highly integrated into regular business operations. The many practical suggestions and examples in this book will rapidly increase your professional abilities, confidence, and effectiveness while shining a spotlight on demonstrable continuous improvements in recovery capability throughout your organization.

I am confident that, through this book, you can master adaptation to the agile world we now live in, provide high value to your organization, and contribute to advancing the profession through actively implementing Adaptive BC.

My deep gratitude to David and Mark for this book, and to all the courageous voices who dare to speak up with new ideas, new approaches, and practical strategies for achieving success in this dynamic, agile environment.

Dan Dorman

Service Continuity Program Manager,
Alaska Airlines
February 2017

Table of Contents

Introduction

The Need for a New Approach: Adaptive Business Continuity

0.1 Why We Wrote This Book

We released "The Continuity 2.0 Manifesto" in September 2015. The manifesto, the continuity20.org website that hosted it, and feedback from readers served as the inspiration for this book. We have since changed the title of the manifesto to the "Adaptive BC Manifesto" and the website to AdaptiveBCP.org to reflect the evolution of thought in preparation for this book.

The manifesto captures and explicates the spirit of the Adaptive Business Continuity (Adaptive BC) approach. It is meant to clearly show how Adaptive BC differs from traditional business continuity (BC) planning. It briefly outlines the approach that the practitioner should take in executing his or her duties, specific practices to avoid, and the overall paradigm that he or she should use in BC planning. The manifesto also defines the values of the Adaptive practitioner and the beginnings of a framework for greatly improving BC practices. It is our hope that this manifesto provides just enough information for practitioners, participants, executives, and academics to begin shaping their own Adaptive BC programs and make needed changes within the profession.

0.2 The Adaptive BC Manifesto in Summary

We encourage you to read the Adaptive BC Manifesto right now! It is included in Appendix B of this book. Table 0-1 summarizes the nine principles of the manifesto. The principles are listed in alphabetical order deliberately to emphasize the fact that no one principle is any more important than another.

0.2.1 Definition

Adaptive Business Continuity (Adaptive BC) is an approach to continuously improve an organization's recovery capabilities, with a focus on the continued delivery of services following an unexpected unavailability of people and/or resources.

0.2.2 Drivers

Despite tremendous revolutions in technology, organizational practice, and global business in the last fifteen years, traditional BC methodology has become stagnant. It has made only small, incremental adjustments, focusing increasingly on compliance and regulations over improvements to organizational readiness. This has led to a progressively untenable state of ineffectual practice, executive disinterest, and an inability to demonstrate the value of continuity programs and practitioners.

0.2.3 Purpose

Adaptive BC transforms or eliminates the majority of traditional instruction and convention in existing best practices of the continuity planning industry. It focuses the discipline and its practitioners on proven practices and away from outdated and ineffectual "best" practices. Adaptive BC better equips continuity practitioners by enhancing their abilities to limit potential damage to an organization's brand, capital, functions, and revenue following an incident or disaster.

0.2.4 Scope

While the principles of Adaptive BC may have implications for information technology disaster recovery, emergency management, life safety, and related fields, they are targeted for the discipline of business continuity. Drawing from the definition, the scope of Adaptive BC:

- Is separate from resilience, sustainability, and other related initiatives.
- Establishes boundaries and guidance for discipline, practice, and critique.
- Provides a framework for ongoing involvement with boards and executives.
- Allows for immediate, innovative, and valuable improvements.

0.2.5 Principles

There are nine principles in the Adaptive BC Manifesto. No single principle takes precedence over any other, nor is there an expected sequence; together the principles should be applied as holistically as possible. They appear in Table 0-1 in alphabetical order.

1. Deliver continuous value.
2. Document only for mnemonics.
3. Engage at many levels within the organization.
4. Exercise for improvement, not for testing.
5. Learn the business.
6. Measure and benchmark.
7. Obtain incremental direction from leadership.
8. Omit the risk assessment and business impact analysis.
9. Prepare for effects, not causes.

Note that we call these "principles." This means they are not specific deliverables or actions. To the extent possible, all nine principles should apply to any activity being performed. When exercising for improvement, for example, the practitioner may use the exercise as an opportunity to measure and benchmark while learning the business and engaging new participants. Exercise activities can even be used to reinforce the use of documents as mnemonics while preparing for effects and not causes.

Table 0-1. Adaptive BC Manifesto Summary Matrix

Deliver continuous value.	Practitioners dictate the work according to sequential methodology and provide documentation at the end of long cycles.	Customers direct the work according to needs and culture; practitioners provide frequent, shorter-term, customer-informed deliverables.
Document only for mnemonics.	Practitioners create documents as final and required deliverables.	Customers create documents as mnemonics.
Engage at many levels within the organization.	N/A. (Practitioners focus buy-in efforts exclusively on executives.)	Practitioners consciously engage many people at many levels of the organization.
Exercise for Improvement, not for testing.	Auditors conduct exercises as a test of the ability to recover within RTO targets.	Departments participate in exercises to practice and improve response and recovery capabilities.
Learn the business.	Practitioners collect data about the business.	Practitioners strive to understand the culture and operations of individual organizational areas.
Measure and benchmark.	Practitioners count the numbers of documents, exercises, and refresh dates.	Practitioners and customers measure preparedness and recoverability.
Obtain incremental direction from leadership.	All executives approve the complete scope of the program before launch.	Individual executives provide iterative direction.
Omit the risk assessment and business impact analysis.	Practitioners require completion of RA and BIA documents before planning can begin.	N/A.
Prepare for effects, not causes.	Experts focus externally: identifying and preparing for a host of specific threats.	Departments focus internally: improving response and recovery capabilities for the unavailability of locations, people, and resources.

0.3 From a Manifesto to a Book

In the months following the original publication of the manifesto, we have had many thoughtful conversations with so many interesting preparedness professionals. There is a desire out there for something new in the profession, some way to reinvigorate our work and free the practitioner from ineffective activities. We have learned a great deal from innovative and creative colleagues who continue to try new solutions in order to deliver value in what they do. A paradigm shift is emerging in BC, one that moves the focus from documentation to preparedness, from compliance to recoverability. Traditional BC seeks to define processes for managing a BC program or system; Adaptive BC seeks to define a framework for preparing organizations to continue business in the event of a disruption. It is a rather subtle difference but the ramifications are significant. This changes the focus from how to effectively manage the teams and mechanisms of BC to how businesses can be better prepared.

Many smart and engaged colleagues across the profession are laying a foundation for this change. The manifesto provided a beginning for reflection and discussion. There is a strong desire for a viable alternative approach to traditional continuity planning. You can hear echoes of it in the writings and postings of many of us, though it lacked a name. We call it Adaptive Business Continuity, and wrote this book to present it more fully to you.

Chapter 1

Demolition

Many stakeholders involved in business continuity (BC) have expressed frustration with the existing state of affairs. Many practitioners feel unrecognized and underappreciated. Executives are confused by our methods and unclear about the value BC professionals provide. Some participants are skeptical of the outcomes and uninterested or frustrated by the activities. And, the discipline as a whole is often unknown to communities at large, despite the fact that costly disasters of every sort increasingly fill our newsfeeds. If you've been involved with this profession for any length of time, then you've likely experienced difficulties yourself or have heard the frequent laments of others.

How did we reach the point where BC is often misunderstood and undervalued? We believe several specific practices in traditional BC are ineffective and should be dismissed. The good news is that a collection of new practices has emerged that has not yet been fully synthesized and adopted. This book is an attempt to bring these practices together within a single framework built on a practical, unifying theory.

This chapter will help you to:

- Recognize specific practices in traditional BC that may be problematic, outdated, or ineffective.
- Identify specific activities that you may wish to eliminate from your practice.
- Approach the BC field with a critical eye and an open mind.
- Consider the need for an alternative approach to continuity planning.

1.1 Demolition: Traditional Practices to Eliminate

This chapter assesses the specific practices in traditional BC that contribute to the frustrations of practitioners, executives, and participants. We have called this chapter "Demolition" because we propose clearing out a space before we can build something new. While the title might seem a bit provocative, we believe this chapter will get you to think about your BC program and the specific practices that might be holding it back.

Take a moment and consider this possibility: Perhaps a main cause of frustrations with BC outcomes is not the way we have gone about executing individual BC activities, but the activities themselves. Perhaps we are expending enormous effort to perform the wrong activities in the right way. We believe this is exactly the case.

Here we provide an analysis of accepted practices within our discipline that we argue no longer meet the needs of today's organizations. These practices are requirements within nearly all BC standards and guides. The details and guidance for each one vary slightly from one institute or association to another but they largely exist with similarly defined objectives and deliverables. Let us look at these practices in-depth to determine if, indeed, they provide value to the overall BC venture. We believe that the following seven traditional practices should be reevaluated or even eliminated in favor of a new, value-driven paradigm:

1. Produce a business impact analysis (BIA).
2. Set recovery time targets.
3. Conduct a risk assessment (RA).
4. Obtain explicit executive support.
5. Document the plan.
6. Test the process.
7. Deliver training and awareness.

1.1.1 Eliminate the Business Impact Analysis

At its core, the BIA is exactly what its name implies: An analysis of the impact to business from a future disastrous event, a process that often proves far easier to state than to actually do. Today's standards go through great pains to explain the steps a practitioner should take to perform just such an analysis. And while standards can vary, they are largely in agreement over some very basic activities that contribute to the final product:

- Identify and define all processes performed within an organization.
- Determine the impact to the organization, in terms of financial loss and inability to meet regulatory and contractual obligations, should each process fail.
- Identify the minimal resources needed to perform each process.
- Prioritize processes across the organization and assign recovery time objectives.
- Identify process dependencies for the purpose of determining downstream impact from the failure of a single process.

Many practitioners add an activity: creation of recovery strategies. As if the BIA was not difficult enough, practitioners create continuity and recovery strategies for each process as part of the BIA itself. This is not the original intent of the BIA, nor is it a recommended practice in any guide or standard; we assert recovery strategies should always be a separate undertaking apart from the BIA. Therefore, we limit the scope of the BIA, for the purposes of our demolition, to its traditional role.

It does not take an exhaustive reading of BC articles and blog posts to see that there are a range of opinions and even doubts about the usefulness and validity of the BIA. The BIA can be said to form the bedrock of traditional BC practices, but it is arguably the most problematic activity. Because others have already gone into detail regarding the many issues associated with the BIA, we briefly outline these arguments in what follows.

1.1.1.1 The BIA Requires Too Much Effort for Too Little Value

A common critique asserts that the BIA requires significant effort with little value to show for it. Jim Mitchell, in his blog for eBRP Solutions, states, "Repeating the pattern of BIA surveying – with its inherent flaws – produces results of little or no value" (Mitchell 2011). The CEO and President of Lootok says the same in his series of articles debunking common myths of BC. Myth #2 in this series is dedicated to the BIA and asks the question "Honestly, what's the point?" leading off with the claim of having "witnessed tons of BIA projects – all exhaustive, but useless from a business perspective." Many commentators and practitioners bemoan the limited return on investment from the often-lengthy effort to produce a BIA.

1.1.1.2 The BIA Becomes Outdated Quickly

Another common concern is that the BIA is a snapshot in time that is so quickly outdated that it is rendered useless (Mitchell, 2011). Given the effort needed to execute a BIA, particularly following the time-consuming requirements in the newest ISO standards (ISO/TS 22317:2015), it stands to reason that information gathered at the start of the process could become stale by its conclusion. Since the results of the BIA form the basis of subsequent activities in traditional BC planning, results could become even further out-of-date as more steps are taken. This creates a potential cycle of misinformation and poor planning. As Mitchell summarizes, "By the time the ink is dry on the Senior Management presentation, the organization has certainly changed. Basing BC and DR [disaster recovery] plans on outdated results compounds the problem" (Mitchell, 2011).

1.1.1.3 The BIA Contains Significant Flaws

In a piece from August 2015, "Lessons Learned from 15 Years of Conducting BIAs," Samuel Shanthan lists twelve individual problems with the BIA. This list summarizes many common complaints, such as overestimating the degree of impact, overstating the importance of individual departments, overlooking critical interdependencies, and the overall subjectivity of the process.

Finally, Rainer Hübert introduces several vital critiques. In his thorough article, "Why the Business Impact Analysis Does Not Work," Hübert (2012) details four major problems with performing a BIA. These are:

Problem 1. The BIA is generally used to confirm assumptions about criticalities, not to identify criticalities. If it would actually be used to correctly identify criticalities, the time and costs needed to apply a BIA would be prohibitive.

Problem 2. The BIA requires an organization with established processes and activity-based costing as part of the day-to-day business to be able to deliver valid, reliable and reproducible information. In reality, only very few organizations can provide that.

Problem 3. The BIA is inaccurate or incomplete in its statement about impacts, since it needs information which is not available at the moment the BIA is created, and consequently either includes assumptions or leaves necessary parts of information out.

Problem 4. The information out of the BIA needs to be aligned against information, which is, in most cases, either not available, or reluctantly provided, or based on quick and dirty problem solving.

Hübert argues that the BIA is ultimately a nonstarter. He sees significant flaws in its approach that render it unreliable and ill advised. Hübert argues, and we agree, that the BIA suffers from both theoretical and practical defects that cannot be overcome. The time and money it would take to accurately identify all processes, their upstream and downstream dependencies, along with a forecasted impact from an unpredictable disaster are likely to be substantial. What specific disaster may befall an organization and the exact scope of its impact is unknowable. Specifying the revenue, liability, regulatory, and even reputational consequences for every function following an unpredictable event and its aftermath is all but impossible. Trying to quantify such an impact is unreasonable. As stated in the second problem of Hübert's paper, "You need an established and consistently implemented system of activity based costing for that…. How many companies actually do have something like that?" (Hübert, 2012). In the end, the BIA has theoretical and practical failings.

1.1.1.4 The BIA Fails When Streamlined

The number of authors and the volume of material written about the BIA and its inherent flaws point to irresolvable problems with the BIA. In response, many practitioners have attempted to "fix" the BIA process. Many advocate for a more concise, streamlined approach, focusing on specific deliverables of the BIA such as prioritizing business functions, defining recovery times, or identifying process dependencies. Some professionals are now trying to save the BIA by eliminating large parts of its scope, picking the activities that are best received in their organization, or trying to keep with its spirit while cutting out many of the recommended activities. We contend that further discussion is fruitless and the entire endeavor should simply be eliminated. We suggest the profession accept the inevitable conclusion that the BIA is defective and must be jettisoned.

Recommendation #1: Omit the BIA

Actually, eliminating the BIA is very good news for the practitioner and our practice. Performing a BIA is unnecessary. You can eliminate it from your BC program and save huge amounts of time, effort, reputational capital, and emotional investment. While we will explain in greater detail throughout the rest of the book, we can summarize our perspective in three points. First, we no longer need a BIA to tell us which parts of the organization are important for planning and recovery. In most cases, senior leadership knows very well what parts of their organization are important. A brief conversation with executives and leadership is likely all you will need to get to work. Second, we no longer need a BIA to prioritize our services. We ought not to prioritize our services at all prior to a disaster, because, as we will discuss in detail later, the order in which leadership decides to recover services following a disaster rightly depends on the post-disaster environment, an evolving situation that cannot be anticipated. And, third, we do not need to set targets for recovery time. This third point leads us into our very next section.

1.1.2 Eliminate Recovery Time Targets

Time is often at the very heart of any discussion of BC and information technology disaster recovery. While planning, practitioners quickly ask, "How soon does it need to be available?" Following a disaster, everyone wants to know, "How soon will it be back up?" Maximum tolerable downtime (MTD), recovery point objective (RPO), recovery time objective (RTO), recovery time capability (RTC), and other time-centric considerations are intertwined within the very nature of current preparedness planning.

But there are deep flaws with the continued attempts to incorporate time into preparedness planning in this manner. These flaws lead to frustrated participants, disengaged managers, wasted effort, and dubious outcomes. Fortunately, these flaws are easily avoidable and correctable.

1.1.2.1 Time Targets Require Inaccessible Information

When the planner asks the participant, "How soon do you need X up and running?" the participant often answers, "It depends." This answer is almost always the most accurate one. How long an organization can do without a particular service or system will depend on factors such as, but not limited to:

- Contracts and legal considerations.
- Current business models, strategic goals, culture, vision, and/or mission of individual departments and the organization overall.
- Estimated time to market or time to launch for in-flight projects and initiatives.
- Influences from the board of directors, shareholders, customers, competitors, and the market.
- Leadership and management priorities.
- Liquidity, capital, and revenue streams.

- Regulations and compliance requirements from federal, state, local, and other regulatory and accrediting bodies.
- The post-disaster status of other organizations affected by the same disaster.
- The post-disaster status of other processes, functions, systems, and services.
- The post-disaster effect on customers, consumers, and end-users of the organization's products and services.
- The time of year, week, or day.
- Simply who happens to be in charge of recovery operations and who is in the war room at any given hour.

Forcing a single answer for recovery time targets may be impossible, inaccurate, and ill advised, because "it depends" is almost always really the best answer.

But, "it depends" is a challenging answer to accept. We want to drive to one specific answer about time, particularly because documenting this answer is required by current practice. Faced with this challenge, we can take a best guess, pick the worst-case scenario, or try to capture all the branching "if/then" conditions that lead to different time requirements. None of these responses seem particularly useful to the organization when planning for or responding to the chaos of an actual disaster.

1.1.2.2 Time Targets Set the Wrong Tone

Practically speaking, the drive to identify and document specific time objectives often gets us off on the wrong foot. We spend a disproportionate amount of effort and reputational capital negotiating with participants to pinpoint these time-related objectives. Frequently the participants, including management, feel that this activity is arbitrary and artificial, searching after something that is unrealistic and unreflective of what would actually happen in the case of disaster. As these conversations often take place at the very beginning of planning work, they can set a negative, and sometimes adversarial, tone to the rest of the planning process.

Since "it depends" is indeed the right answer, there is a related problem with our determination to define a single time within which to recover a given service: It is inflexible. Once designated, such times rarely, if ever, change. The designated time then becomes the default measure by which all other activities are validated. It drives the recovery procedures and the objectives of all subsequent testing. It is often the first factor to be considered when events occur that do disrupt service, the consequence of which is that recovery time objectives become some of the first casualties.

1.1.2.3 Time Targets Create Risk Through Faulty Estimates

Recovery times are arguably the single most dominant values in an organization's entire continuity program. Likely only a small number of mature BC programs do not capture recovery time targets. Consequently, establishing a recovery time for services is perhaps the most central activity of the practitioner in traditional continuity planning, usually in conjunction with the BIA. This is a particularly troubling situation if, as we have argued, recovery time targets and recovery time estimates are flawed from the outset.

Certainty can be a good thing. But certainty arrived at through spurious means is a serious risk. As has been demonstrated previously, the BIA is far from perfect. Using such a subjective and ill-suited tool to arrive at something so fixed is asking for trouble. Inaccurate time targets can forever set a practitioner's program down the wrong path. Focusing on time targets can misguide planning participants, and shift resources from more important efforts, such as actually increasing recovery capabilities. Worse still, inaccurate estimates of recovery capabilities can set a false sense of security which could prove catastrophic following a disaster.

1.1.2.4 Time Targets Embody Significant Flaws

These are by no means the only challenges involved in trying to establish recovery time targets. Other significant problems are:

- The inability to accurately predict what specific disaster will happen and what the actual effects of that disaster will be (Hübert, 2012).
- The inability to fully encapsulate and accurately map out all functions and interdependencies for each service (Hübert, 2012).
- The framing of exercises as artificial tests of recovery time instead of opportunities to identify strengths to reinforce and gaps to close.
- The inability of a department to properly estimate the criticality of their services within the larger context and mission of the entire organization (Hatton, Grimshaw, Vargo, & Seville, 2016; Hübert, 2012).
- The tendency of a department to (consciously or unconsciously) inflate and over-estimate the criticality of their services (Hatton et al., 2016; Hübert, 2012; Shanthan, 2015).
- The protracted amount of time it takes to decide on and document time targets, particularly in comparison to the relative return on investment (Murphy, 2016).
- The likelihood that documented time targets will be unable to keep pace with continuous changes to the organization, staffing, marketplace, regulations, suppliers, business drivers, local and global conditions, and so forth.

> ### Recommendation #2: Do Not Set Time Targets
>
> In the face of these problems, the professional must seriously question whether identifying and documenting targets of time provides value, and if the current approach to time has been misguided from the beginning. This may be a daunting proposition. Many of us, the authors included, find it quite challenging to disentangle time objectives from the heart of BC. But we believe such a separation can and must be done.
>
> Our approach to time in BC planning must be completely rethought, refined, and refocused, leading to a new approach that will solve the problems but look very little like our traditional practices. As we will see in the next chapter, time in preparedness planning is not a target, but one of three constraints. It is the job of the preparedness planner to identify and document all three constraints, not just time. Those in charge of recovery need to know how much money they can spend, how much time they can take, and to what degree of functionality a service must be restored.

1.1.3 Eliminate the Risk Assessment

BC is not a risk management (RM) discipline. The focus of BC is not the management and mitigation of risk but preparation for the possible materialization of a threat. BC is predicated on the assumption that not all risks can be predicted or controlled. Surprisingly, then, if you look at any publication, website, or blog devoted to BC, you will find a large proportion of the content dedicated to RM. Most practitioners make the mistake of thinking that RM is a responsibility within the BC discipline, that the two activities are one-and-the-same, or that they are somehow intertwined. But we believe this is a serious misunderstanding. Not only is it a distraction but it robs precious time and resources from BC efforts.

1.1.3.1 RM Belongs to an Entirely Different Discipline

RM is a discipline with its own methodology and practices. It has experts within its domain who are very adept at the practice of RM. We assert that the risk assessment is one activity that should remain within the purview of RM, not undertaken by BC practitioners. Instead of riding on the coattails of RM we should be establishing the need for BC as a separate, distinct, and equally important endeavor from RM.

RM, as a discipline, is relatively mature. It is used throughout organizations in making strategic, operational, and financial decisions. As an instrument for contributing to the bottom line, RM practices are widely accepted. Not so for BC which is comparatively young and continues to struggle for widespread legitimacy. This leads to a significant disparity between the resources and effort devoted to RM in comparison to BC at many organizations. Treating BC as another RM activity often results in the diversion of scarce resources away from BC activities to further RM efforts.

1.1.3.2 RM Takes Time Away from Valuable BC Tasks

Time devoted to preventing loss is time taken away from improving recoverability from loss, and vice versa. You can devote equal time to each but more time dedicated to one is time taken away from the other. RM is the business of identifying, categorizing, and controlling risks; this is an important endeavor but does not necessarily contribute directly to making an organization more prepared to effectively respond to the outages it does experience. Effective RM is not just about mitigating risks but also accepting, transferring, or remediating known risks. Therefore, RM itself recognizes the fact that risks can still materialize. It is the BC professional's job to help prepare the organization to effectively and efficiently recover should a risk eventually materialize.

1.1.3.3 RM May Not Keep Pace with Global Complexities

The world and its global economy have become incredibly complex. Many events that have had the largest impact on businesses and communities did not arise from isolated threats, but were the result of cascading combinations of complex events. As Nassim Nicholas Taleb (2007) argued in his renowned book on risk, *The Black Swan: The Impact of the Highly Improbable*, many disasters are caused by events that were thought to be improbable to the point of impossible. Arguably, the terrorist attacks of September 11, 2001 and the global financial collapse of 2007-2008 are recognized examples of black swan events. In fact, many RM practitioners question whether its traditional techniques pass muster in a world of such complexity.

In a 2016 article, "The Rise of Complex Risk Theory, and How Traditional Risk Management Practices Will Need to Evolve in Order to Survive in an Agile World," Warren Black states that "many of the industry accepted management models and historically accepted operating paradigms are no longer suited to the needs of a significantly more connected, dynamic and agile world," arguing that "environments of advanced complexity and uncertainty require risk management solutions that are significantly more holistic and adaptive (agile)...." What Black says about RM is true for BC: "...the vast majority of existing operating models are designed to suit a more structured and stable world of lower complexity and higher certainty rather than the highly dynamic, fluid and agile world we are currently experiencing" (Black, 2016).

Ironically, this approach of focusing on RM to the detriment of recoverability presents a risk in and of itself. It reduces the resources needed to adequately prepare for the impact and downtime associated with unmitigated threats. Because threats can still materialize for a variety of reasons, organizations must devote time and effort to preparedness work or run the risk of being unable to effectively respond and recover from actual disruptions. In some cases, the outcome is even worse: When leaders are convinced that RM addresses all potential issues through mitigation and insurance, they may be lulled into a false sense of security that can put their entire organization at risk of being able to survive a catastrophic event.

> **Recommendation #3: Leave Out the Risk Assessment**
> We believe that you would be wise to eliminate the risk assessment from your work as a BC professional. Unless you are a specialist in both disciplines, focus on the strengths and value you provide within the domain of preparedness and recoverability. While the risk manager works to prevent risks from occurring, you work to prepare the organization to recover when they do materialize. It may very well be your work that ultimately saves the organization from disaster.

1.1.4 Eliminate Explicit Executive Support

Few activities in the collective BC canon are as widely promoted as the need for executive support. In almost all written work and every presentation on the subject of BC, executive buy-in for the program is touted as one of the most critical factors to success from the outset. The common mantra within the discipline is that, without this crucial first-step, the entire endeavor is jeopardized. Obtaining upfront executive approval is therefore specified as a necessary activity within nearly all documented practices.

1.1.4.1 Explicit Executive Support Is Not Required in Other Professions

It seems odd that, before beginning work on improving an organization's preparedness, the BC practitioner must first, "identify products and services *and all related activities* within the scope of the BCMS [business continuity management system]" (ISO 22301, Section 4.3.2 [authors' emphasis]). At that point, the practitioner is directed to take the step of engaging executive leadership before any meaningful BC activity such as analysis, planning, or implementation begins. Standards require the practitioner to obtain explicit approval for the program's vision and all the commensurate activities that are to be undertaken in fulfillment of the program's mission and objectives. BC is uncharacteristic among many other professions in being charged to obtain so much up-front approval from so many people before it can begin to deliver value. Bank supervisors do not need to go to their senior management for permission to make use of tellers. Lawyers do not need to explain the overall benefits of the legal field to CEOs before they help avoid costly litigation. Why should we assume that BC lacks support until one goes specifically to request it?

1.1.4.2 Explicit Executive Support Adds Unnecessary Redundancy and Risk

This executive-approval-first approach puts BC leaders in the unenviable position not only of having to educate top management about BC and getting their buy-in for their program's objectives, but also to ensure that the C-suite will commit to being champions for BC! We could well imagine that if every function of the organization needed so much support, the company might collapse from the overhead.

For example, standard ISO 22301:2012 exhorts top management to undertake 17 separate steps to "demonstrate leadership and commitment with respect to the BCMS [BC Management System]." In Section 5.2, top management is asked to demonstrate their commitment to a BC program by "ensuring the integration of… [BC] requirements into the organization's business processes," "communicating the importance of... conforming to the BCMS requirements," "ensuring that the BCMS achieves its intended outcome(s)," and "directing and supporting persons to contribute to the effectiveness of the BCMS," among other actions. It seems unrealistic not only to dictate that "top management and other relevant management roles… *shall* demonstrate leadership with respect to the BCMS" (Section 5.1 [authors' emphasis]), but that it is accomplished before planning can even begin!

Whether it is a consultant, a contractor, a dedicated employee, or a whole team that performs BC functions, it must be acknowledged that, at some point, someone within the organization saw fit to devote capital and resources to BC. Turning around to request support, outline every activity, request executives' commitment, line up champions, and obtain permission to do the work you were hired to do is simply redundant. Worse still, it puts the practitioner on the defensive from the outset, threatening everyone's credibility if not executed effectively. Executives, managers, and frontline staff may begin to wonder why the BC program needs so much up-front support before any work can begin.

We do not mean to imply that executives should not be informed nor are we suggesting that funding is unnecessary. Work will still require resources and any sizable action will need to be communicated for awareness and to address management concerns. But such endeavors should follow normal protocols; doing otherwise is wasteful. It also could create an environment in which the BC practitioner must work outside of normal, established channels to get things done. This can give leaders the impression that the BC function cannot work within such parameters or that its practitioners require more handholding and direction.

An executive may well ask, "What kind of an undertaking is this if it will fail without my up-front and continuous support?"

1.1.4.3 Explicit Executive Support Is Not Required for Success

Conventional BC wisdom assumes that if the practitioner cannot obtain leadership buy-in, then all BC activities will be made more difficult. But there is no evidence that this is so. Just as one does not assume that executives will issue directives about BC and thereby miraculously remove all obstacles to planning, there is also no need to think they will put up roadblocks if they have not been given the opportunity to provide their explicit blessing. In fact, many practitioners create successful BC programs that have been run from the ground up. Such approaches leverage word of mouth, positive peer pressure, quick wins, and delivery of tangible benefits to build momentum and gain traction. Some programs are successful in part because they "fly under the radar," operating with a small budget to produce genuine business value. The real effort needed to build preparedness capabilities is the same whether one has approached their organization's senior management or not.

Even assuming the BC professional obtains full, enthusiastic support up-front, what then? Does this automatically ensure the smooth execution of a BC program? There is often an implicit assumption in traditional BC practice that executive support translates into backing and cooperation throughout the organization, clearing the path for the planner and eliminating the need for further persuasion and justification. Yet with or without visible executive support the real work of BC usually takes place far from the C-suite. BC leaders and teams must still do the heavy lifting needed to obtain relevant information, engage managers, supervisors, and individuals, and drive recovery capability improvements. Support is required at all levels of the organization. Engagement and information from middle management and individual contributors is equally important. An approving vote from the CFO probably doesn't even register with the finance team five floors below.

1.1.4.4 Explicit Executive Support Does Not Meet Executives' Priority for Action

The executive-support-first approach does not speak to corporate leaders' concerns or priorities. This up-front tactic takes up valuable time with leaders by attempting to educate, define a vision, and build a case for leadership oversight and support. It is not action oriented, leaving many a C-level individual with a sense that nothing has been accomplished despite the time dedicated to the endeavor. There are three reasons an up-front requirement for support causes problems particularly between executives and practitioners:

1. **Executives want to talk business value.** Yes, BC can provide a competitive advantage and there are consequences to not meeting regulatory or contractual obligations. But leaders want to know what they are buying. How will this endeavor contribute to the bottom line or minimize the organization's exposure to specific risks? If investment is needed then what is the return? If there is time needed from individuals throughout the organization, what will be the results of such effort? What will be delivered, not just in terms of documents or materials, but in terms of value? Using existing standards as a guide, planners are driven to speak conceptually about possible threats and their potential consequences, adding a sprinkling of scare tactics as needed, then launching into their vision for policies, roles, meetings, governance, templates, committees, and documentation. Under traditional practices, planners are exhorted to tell executives what they should want and how they need to support a specific approach to create specific products and materials. And we wonder why executives are not more enthusiastic about BC!

2. **Top management is pressed for time.** Regardless of the actual best practice guide one explicitly follows, the expectation is clear: Traditional BC requires the practitioner to conduct a formal activity whereby executives are educated about the importance of BC and informed of the details of the program and its

implementation. This is redundant, as mentioned above, since the hiring of any BC resource demonstrates the organization's support for the endeavor. Without having concrete data about the program and the business value it provides, precious time is spent presenting ideas and explaining the components of the program. In many corporate-driven activities, executives do not feel the need to be informed of the details. And what is true for one executive is more so for an entire steering committee.

3. **Perhaps most importantly, executives want to hear and see action.** Defining and presenting a vision sounds lofty and important but does nothing to improve recoverability. Leaders want to know what you've accomplished, what you plan on doing next, and what you need them to do. This means taking up their time only when you have explicit decisions to make or obstacles to remove. If you have an objective that requires corporate leaders to take action, be clear about what it is, when it should be done, and what value it will ultimately provide. Presenting to a boardroom full of leaders about the importance of BC and detailed plans for its implementation is not worthwhile. Most leaders are likely to leave such meetings without a much-needed sense of action and accomplishment.

Recommendation #4: Obtain Only the Executive Support You Need

It is easy to see why executive support has occupied such an oversized position in our practice as well as among practitioners. It is an easy scapegoat for many of our current woes. This single activity has been promoted as the linchpin upon which all future success will hinge. And, to an extent, our existing practices are set up to make it that way. But practitioners have stood up successful programs without this step while other programs have certainly suffered and failed despite near-universal support from the organization's C-suite. Corporate visions and mission statements should be part of a good BC practitioner's arsenal. We need to use executive discussion as an opportunity to speak to business value and specific action items. We must get out of the executive education business and get into the business of learning what is important to leaders as well as what makes business sense.

1.1.5 Eliminate Requirements to Document the Plan

BC standards, practices, and even job postings emphasize the need to create "the plan" that addresses all BC needs, written in detail. When disaster strikes, most folks in the organization expect that someone will pull out "the plan" and handle the situation. Yet, evidence points to significant problems with an approach that focuses on documented plans. There are a slew of articles, case studies, and supporting research that detail the problems surrounding the use of written documentation in a post-disaster environment. For the purposes of this book, let us limit our discussion to the main problem with documented BC plans: Written plans can prove inaccurate and unhelpful when responding to disaster.

1.1.5.1 Documented Plans Grow Increasingly Useless with Time

Ironically, most BC practitioners already recognize the problems inherent in documented plans. Many decades ago, 19th century German military strategist Helmuth von Moltke the Elder reportedly said that "no plan of operations extends with any certainty beyond the first contact with the main hostile force." This is often paraphrased as "no plan survives first contact with the enemy" and is a common refrain in BC circles. Get involved with BC for even a few days and you will inevitably hear or read a quote to the effect that any plan developed prior to an event is all but useless in its immediate aftermath. The fact is that it is impossible to document a detailed set of procedures that will enable a group of individuals to effectively respond to any and all post-disaster situations.

There is no such thing as the perfect plan. Documented plans are most effective the moment they are written and only grow significantly more useless with each passing day. The very sad part is that BC practitioners already know this. They admit it and even write and present on the subject. But then many of us continue to develop documented plans anyway.

1.1.5.2 Documented Plans Are a Poor Fit for the Task

Even if a useful plan could be documented in detail and kept accurate, few people are likely to look at it when disaster strikes. Folks are apt to forget that these documents even exist as binders are quickly relegated to a dusty shelf once they are produced. Sometimes employees cannot find the plans or access them electronically should an actual disaster happen. Even making a documented plan available in the cloud or via smart devices – regardless of format – is no guarantee anyone will read it ahead of time or think to look at it following a disaster. The practitioner quickly becomes a bother by constantly reminding people of where their plans are located and how to access them should a disaster occur.

Furthermore, people often do not want to use documents or, worse, are psychologically unable to use them. This is why sports, military, airline, and other industries spend so much time drilling and exercising their people. Post-disaster situations place so much psychological and physical stress on the brain, significantly limiting one's ability for cognitive thought, such that people react out of habit, not because they are reading documented instructions.

1.1.5.3 Documented Plans Grow Too Long and Detailed

Some plans are monstrous in length, documents so heavy with scale, scope, objectives, assumptions, roles, responsibilities, approvals, and tracked changes that the actual recovery procedures become buried. Often times even the procedures are so gargantuan as to require more time to read through than to execute. They often include irrelevant details about building evacuation or responding to a bomb threat as if the document is intuitively the first place the average worker will turn when a fire alarm goes off or they pick up the phone to be given an ultimatum. In a study of organizations following the 2011 Canterbury, New Zealand earthquakes, researchers found that in more than one organization, "while their plan was quite thorough, too much of the detail was presented and this made it very difficult for employees on the ground to quickly find the relevant information. The large amount of information presented actually hindered employees' ability to access the information they needed" (Hatton et al., 2016, p. 88). These are usually the plans that easily pass regulatory and audit inspections but are of little use otherwise.

Software tools do not solve, and sometimes exacerbate, these problems. Such tools can ensure that documented plans are of a consistent format and contain a certain amount of data within each section. They can be pre-populated by the BC practitioner. They can be searchable and the data quickly replaceable. They can pull information from relevant sources and tie it back to the defined strategy. But at the end of the day, the result is often a long, printable document with sentence after sentence that the BC practitioner expects regular employees to follow in a stressful and chaotic post-disaster situation. As the Canterbury earthquake study concludes, "Planning for a crisis does not mean writing a plan" (Hatton et al., 2016, pp. 89-90).

1.1.5.4 Documented Plans Distract from Real Purpose

There is one last, subtle, and vital reason not to create "the plan." A focus on documentation gives the organization a kind of tunnel vision to see BC planning in terms of documents. It sets the misperception that documenting information is the essence of preparedness. This shifts the focus almost entirely to procedures and away from the resources and crisis competencies that are so important in any recovery. Document-driven approaches concentrate on writing down recovery strategy scripts, BIA results, inventory lists, and the like. This largely ignores the importance of putting the right resources in place before the disaster, and improving the psychological competencies necessary for employees to function during a crisis. It also reduces flexibility and innovation at time of disaster, as people will look to do what is written down for them instead of engaging in creative problem solving to address a shifting post-disaster environment. Documenting the plan can lead to a very myopic approach to preparedness.

Recommendation #5: Use Dashboards Not Documents

These problems with documented plans are no reason for despair. In fact, by giving up the need to create "the plan" for disaster, the BC practitioner can focus on a fuller and more valuable set of improvements to better equip the organization to recover. We will provide an alternate approach as we explain Adaptive BC in later chapters. For the time being, remember our friend Helmuth von Moltke the Elder as well as this oft cited quote from Eisenhower: "In preparing for battle I have always found that plans are useless, but planning is indispensable."

1.1.6 Eliminate Requirements to Test the Process

Testing often forms the capstone of our BC programs. Many call it "exercising" but in the majority of cases it is actually a test. Why? Because it comes near the end of the traditional BC planning lifecycle and carries with it the expectation that participants will recover specific systems or functions within the predetermined timeframe exactly in line with what is written in the plan. That is a test. A test indicates whether participants can follow established procedures within set parameters. While an exercise allows for adaptation in response to different scenarios and situations, a test is largely a yes or no verdict on the content of a documented plan and the ability of employees to follow it.

Test v. Exercise: It should be noted that most common standards (ISO 22301, DRI International's *Professional Practices*, and NFPA 1600) use the terms *exercise* and *test* interchangeably. Some even list them together as "exercise/test," further supporting the notion that the two are one and the same. Because of this, we will use the term *test* from here on out to refer to traditional BC practices and *exercise* as it relates to Adaptive Business Continuity (Adaptive BC).

There are three significant problems with our profession's approach to testing; we will discuss each in turn below:

1. Testing reinforces the concept of time as an objective and plans as scripts.
2. Testing drives participants to meet the objective, not to improve recoverability.
3. Testing wastes opportunities to make meaningful improvement.

1.1.6.1 Testing Reinforces the Concept of Time as an Objective and Plans as Scripts

As we detailed previously, time should not be an objective in recovery planning. Many current approaches attempt to define a sequence of planning activities, then place testing at the end of all BC work. This only reinforces the notion that testing is tied to time. This is a natural consequence of our traditional approach to BC. Particularly when testing, we strive to distill our efforts down to a very simple and easily digestible metric: time. Time is clear, consistent, and universally understood. As such, it makes for an easy testing objective. This makes the ultimate measure of a test much easier, by asking: Can the service recover within the prescribed timeframe? But as we have seen, time targets are misleading and should be eliminated from BC planning.

There is a secondary – sometimes less explicit – objective in testing: checking to see how well participants will follow their plans. In this respect, testing is thought to serve as a validation of business recovery "scripts." As with time, this provides both an easy measure going into the activity as well as a simple objective at the conclusion of the test: update the documented plan. But this approach fails on three levels:

1. **It is nearly impossible to confirm the ability of employees to follow the written script during the chaos of an actual disaster.** It is one thing to talk through a script in the comfort of a conference room; it is quite another to follow documented instructions in the aftermath of death and destruction.
2. **It lacks a way to measure outcomes.** Given the vast numbers of potential disaster situations and black swan risks, how could we judge whether following the script would achieve the desired recovery outcomes?
3. **Past performance is not always a good predictor of future results when it comes to following written instructions.** As we discussed above, plans are not perfect and users cannot be depended upon to even find their plans when the time comes. During a test, there is a clear incentive to follow the script, but at time of disaster, any person may decide that there are more important steps to take and thus ignore the documented plan.

1.1.6.2 Testing Drives Participants to Meet the Objective, Not to Improve Recoverability

This brings us to the second serious problem with our traditional scripted approach to testing: the incentive to take shortcuts to meet stated objectives. There is a clear expectation among participants that they will perform a very specific set of actions within a very definite period of time. Failure to do so runs the risk of the endeavor being labeled a failure along with any negative consequences such as having to perform the entire activity all over again. This is clearly something everyone wants to avoid – the BC planner included. The incentive, therefore, is to get this work done within the time established.

These incentives can make the entire process suspect from the start:

- **There is the incentive to hit the set time targets, no matter how.** This is not to say that testing participants are making a conscious effort to cheat. By and large the individuals involved in this activity have been engaged in other BC related efforts and wish to see the positive results of their work. But when the clock starts ticking it can be all too tempting to skip a step, take a shortcut, stick with the script even though it might not make sense, or to make assumptions and move on, all in the interest of delivering on the objective: to recover within the defined timeframe. Participants may encounter questions or concerns with the procedures in front of them but move on in the interest of speeding through the recovery test. Errors may pop up that are simply ignored because doing otherwise threatens the stated objective of the test. Participants may skip over items they know will result in questionable results. In short, there is a real risk that genuine problems will be overlooked, missed, or even deliberately hidden in an effort to demonstrate compliance with the defined recovery time requirement.

- **Even the BC planner is incentivized to circumvent problems in order to deliver a positive report card to senior management**. Again, this does not have to be a conscious attempt at deception. Such actions may be easily justified during recovery as being inconsequential to the result. Planners and participants alike may genuinely intend to revisit such problems post-exercise or to raise them in the final report. But this does not change the fact that the results of the test may not be fully accurate.

- **BC leadership and the entire approach itself may conspire to create an environment in which shortcuts are tacitly encouraged and problems avoided.** Tests are scheduled well in advance in order to provide adequate time and effort to prepare. The ticking clock may not even be started until all participants have been mobilized, in place, and ready to execute. This creates an impression that the effort is fabricated, not for the purpose of identifying and correcting potential problems, but of removing any potential obstacles to meeting the recovery time. As long as the overarching objective is met, most every problem encountered as part of the exercise is easily forgotten or glossed over; but these are exactly the problems that could cause significant costs and complications in an actual disaster. Once the test is complete and it is confirmed that the available time has not been exceeded, everyone breathes a collective sigh of relief. Effort will be devoted to debrief sessions and lessons learned but once the final report is delivered most issues will have been relegated to ancient history.

1.1.6.3 Testing Wastes Opportunities to Make Meaningful Improvement

This leads us to the third and, by far, the most serious consequence of testing that is focused on documentation and time targets: Many meaningful lessons that could be gleaned from the testing process are lost. Testing that focuses on adherence to a predetermined script will necessarily eliminate discussion and exploration of other alternatives. Testing documented procedures will not allow for thinking of new and effective ways to solve problems, whether those problems are known or are encountered during the course of working through a scenario. The ability to empower employees to critically solve emerging problems and thereby improve recovery capabilities is ignored.

This means the loss of many potential benefits of an effective exercise approach. Barriers to effective recovery can be missed or deliberately overlooked when there is no incentive to do otherwise. Lessons-learned meetings become an activity to perform after the recovery rather than using the exercise itself as an opportunity to learn. We often create an artificial environment in which printed plans are provided to our participants rather than relying on what would normally be available or instinctive for them in a real scenario. This is compounded by the fact that we set up the entire endeavor as something to be passed rather than an opportunity to understand and improve.

Exercising, by contrast, provides an opportunity for participants to do what comes naturally. Performed properly, BC practitioners can observe and work jointly with those involved to make corrections and improvements during the exercise. Without the risk of failure, an exercise can be executed without judgment. This frees those involved to raise issues and problems then work towards solutions. Furthermore, exercises reinforce good practices. Replacing the compulsory regimen of periodical testing, together with its resource-intensive planning efforts, with less controlled exercise activities promotes flexibility and frees up bandwidth to exercise more frequently. This only increases the opportunities to develop proper response behaviors and identify corrective actions.

Recommendation #6: Exercise Instead of Test

While we will leave it up to you to decide, we believe that tests should be eliminated in favor of thoughtful exercises. Exercises do not have to come at the end of all planning activities. They do not have to be time bound, nor do they have to be assigned a grade or an objective to meet. The benefit of exercises is that they can be as basic or as difficult as necessary. Exercising provides opportunities to identify problems and to exceed expectations. We will discuss exercising within the Adaptive BC approach later in the book.

1.1.7 Eliminate Standalone Training and Awareness

Usually, the very last step in the traditional BC planning lifecycle is the delivery of training and awareness. This is a rather strange suggestion when you think about it. Shouldn't training and awareness be ongoing activities woven into the entire planning process? And why would BC practitioners be the ones to provide training if they aren't the experts on how to recover specific services? Finally, given that the delivery of training and awareness requires soft skills and specialized knowledge, is the BC practitioner actually equipped with the skills to do this well?

1.1.7.1 Traditional Training and Awareness Belong to a Separate Discipline

Our discipline's approach to training and awareness is not unlike its approach to RM. Training is a separate, specialized activity that is nonetheless assigned to the BC planner or team to do. Like RM, training is a discipline unto itself with methodologies, a body of knowledge, experts, and certifications. Despite how complex the recovery procedures or how short a time period is allowed for execution, planners expect that they can train others despite the fact that they are experts neither in training nor the service to be recovered. It begs the question why BC planners feel the need to take this endeavor on entirely by themselves rather than leveraging the expertise that may exist in marketing, communications, or other related areas.

This traditional approach turns training and awareness into a standalone product to be delivered rather than something intrinsic to the process. Training comes at the end of a planning lifecycle, oftentimes rushed through to meet deadlines. Awareness activities are often ignored or relegated to a few readily available posters. These are ineffectual practices at best, and potentially negligent ones at worst.

1.1.7.2 Traditional Training and Awareness Pose a Significant Challenge to Measuring the Benefits

The traditional approach to training and awareness also ignores the fundamental problem of measuring this step. Traditionally, planners as well as auditors and regulators merely look for evidence that training has been delivered. But where is the proof that the training provided the intended benefit? Good measurement of learning seeks to confirm a change in behavior as a result. But within BC, such changes are sometimes assumed without any verification. This is largely a consequence of BC practitioners taking on training activities without a proper understanding of training principles or experience in the training discipline. BC planners make the erroneous assumption that their in-depth knowledge of BC makes them qualified to train, but in-depth knowledge of a subject does not make one particularly effective at educating others about it. Training is a discipline unto itself and requires a good degree of skill and experience to perform properly.

1.1.7.3 Traditional Training and Awareness Occur Too Late in the Process

Furthermore, because training and awareness typically occur at the very end of the traditional BC lifecycle, there is the threat that the entire planning process will have to be started from scratch if significant problems are encountered at this phase. The traditional lifecycle approach dictates that we develop and implement strategies, then create and test plans so that everything can finally be handed off and presented in a formal training session. What of the participant who now questions the validity of the plans or points out a fundamentally flawed assumption? Having gone through the entire planning process it is very likely that the practitioner will dismiss such critical input. If not, then everyone must start the entire process over based on the newly acquired knowledge.

Recommendation #7: Integrate Training and Awareness

A better approach involves learning what is known, understood, and instinctual from representatives across the organization. From there, the practitioner can build on existing competencies and make minor modifications to established approaches. Frequent exercises can be used to re-enforce new skills and knowledge. This makes participants active members of the process instead of a captive and silent audience, and ensures that improvements have the intended benefits. Effective metrics, properly employed, can gauge the improvements to individual and group competencies. This should be the objective of a disciplined approach to training: improved skills and abilities, not simply validation that a given presentation has been attended.

1.2 Conclusion: Eliminate These Practices for a New Approach

This chapter opened with the question, "How did we reach the point where BC is often so misunderstood and undervalued?" We believe the foregoing arguments show conclusively that specific practices in traditional BC are ineffective and should be dismissed. In this chapter, we presented a list of traditional BC practices that we feel are causing more harm than good and need to be eliminated. These seven practices are widely accepted, adopted, and implemented on a daily basis, yet flawed. They are not only detrimental to practitioners, participants, and the profession, but many have inherent theoretical and practical failings that render them nonstarters.

Why did we take the time and effort to detail these shortcomings of the BC profession? We needed to clear a path for what we believe is a better approach to BC planning. Before we could propose our recommendations, we needed to make it unambiguously clear that many existing practices cannot simply be tweaked for improvement. These seven core practices that make up the heart of traditional continuity planning must be "demolished" to make way for improvement.

While you may find it surprising, we believe this is all very good news for anyone involved in BC planning. Traditional BC practices are frequently very inefficient. Their continued execution reinforces a situation where practitioners are misunderstood, executives are confused, participants are bored, and the profession is undervalued. By eliminating these practices from your BC program, you will save time, effort, money, and resources. You will do a lot more with what you have, and get more of the recognition you deserve as you deliver business value in rapid iterations.

In Chapter 4, we provide you with five different narratives that show what it might be like as a successful Adaptive BC practitioner with satisfied executives and engaged participants. Adaptive BC offers a robust alternative to traditional continuity planning, one that operates without the problematic activities discussed above, and provides a strong theoretical foundation for effective practices.

We believe that an alternate approach, the Adaptive BC framework, can provide dramatic improvements in BC. Let us introduce this framework to you now.

References

Black, W. (2016). *The rise of complex risk theory, and how traditional risk management practices will need to evolve in order to survive in an agile world.* Retrieved from https://www.linkedin.com/pulse/rise-complex-risk-theory-how-traditional-management-practices-black?

DRI International. (2014, July). *Professional practices for business continuity practitioners.* New York, NY: Author.

Hatton, T., Grimshaw, E., Vargo, J., & Seville, E. (2016). Lessons from disaster: Creating a business continuity plan that really works. *Journal of Business Continuity and Emergency Planning, 10*(1), 84-92.

Hübert, R. (2012). Why the business impact analysis does not work. *The Business Continuity and Resiliency Journal, 1*(2), 31-39.

International Organization for Standardization (ISO). (2012). *ISO 22301:2012 Societal security – Business continuity management systems – Requirements.* Geneva, Switzerland: Author.

International Organization for Standardization (ISO). (2015). *ISO/TS 22317:2015 Societal security – Business continuity management systems – Guidelines for business impact analysis (BIA).* Geneva, Switzerland: Author.

Mitchell, J. (2011, December 9). *The BIA survey – An effort in futility.* Retrieved from https://www.ebrp.net/the-bia-survey-an-effort-in-futility/

Murphy, S. (2015, August 7). *Myth #2: You need a business impact analysis.* Retrieved from http://lootok.com/assets/uploads/misc/lootok-myth-2-20150807.pdf

National Fire Protection Association (NFPA). (2016). *NFPA 1600: Standard on disaster/emergency management and business continuity/continuity of operations programs.* Quincy, MA: Author.

Shanthan, S. (2015, August 27). *Lessons learned from 15 years of conducting BIAs.* Retrieved from http://www.continuitycentral.com/index.php/news/business-continuity-news/460-lessons-learned-from-15-years-of-conducting-bias

Taleb, N. N. (2007). *The black swan: The impact of the highly improbable.* New York, NY: Random House.

Chapter 2

Foundation

While, to date, best practices, good practices, regulations, and standards are available for continuity planning, we agree with researcher Camilla Amundsen that no single model exists to bring together all of their various recommended activities (2014, p.18). In this book, we aim to remedy this deficit by way of what we call the *capability and constraint model of recoverability*. We believe this model establishes an integrated theoretical foundation for all work related to continuity planning, and offers a solid basis for the daily practice of preparedness professionals.

In this chapter, we begin by defining a few terms and delineating a proper scope for the model. Next, we provide a full overview of the model and show how it provides a powerful platform upon which to build an effective business continuity (BC) program. We then discuss the proper use of time in Adaptive Business Continuity (Adaptive BC), moving from a conception of time as a target to time as a constraint. In the remaining sections of this chapter, we go into more detail about each portion of the model and provide additional examples. If you are interested in the mechanics of measuring preparedness and recoverability in detail, we have included additional material in Appendix A. By laying a foundation for Adaptive BC through the *capability and constraint model of recoverability* in this chapter, we prepare you for step-by-step procedures in Chapter 3 and narrative examples in Chapter 4.

Note that this chapter is more theoretical and academic in tone than the other chapters in the book. Such detail is necessary given the goal of establishing an integrated foundation for the Adaptive BC approach in the industry and your work.

This chapter will help you to:
- Identify the principles that define recoverability in the context of this work.
- Recognize what is, and is not, included in the scope of the Adaptive BC framework.
- Learn the capability and constraint model of recoverability.
- Identify and differentiate between six types of constraints and three types of capabilities.
- Understand how to use time as a constraint and not a target.
- Further understand the model by means of a detailed example.

2.1 Context: Setting the Stage

Providing the correct context for BC work is vital. What is the ultimate purpose of BC and what value does it provide? In what ways should BC be considered a profession? How should the professional spend his or her time, for what reason, and to what end? How will *you* answer these questions when you are sitting in front of the board of directors or in your boss's office? Because BC has been based on a largely disparate collection of activities and not on a firm foundation of integrated theory, these types of questions have proved to be difficult to answer.

One challenge of BC discussions is that critical concepts in this industry are still unclear or undefined. Terms such as *resilience, continuity planning, sustainability, disaster recovery, survivability, risk management* and others are often equated or conflated. By briefly defining a few terms and principles up front, we establish the scope of this chapter to establish a working definition of *recoverability* and establish the boundaries for what is ahead.

We begin by setting forth four principles:
1. Preparing for recovery is not prevention.
2. Recoverability is not survivability or resilience.
3. Recoverability concerns recovery from a physical and/or staffing loss.
4. Recoverability concerns the reestablishment of services, either individually or as an organic whole.

2.1.1 First Principle: Preparing for Recoverability Is Not Prevention

First off, *recoverability* must be differentiated from *prevention*. This point is often lost, confused, or conflated, so we state it here as a clear principle.

No matter how much an organization has worked to mitigate risks in an attempt to prevent an incident, it may be forced to recover from loss. A building may have the finest environmental alarms, fire suppression systems, closed circuit monitors, security systems, vehicle blockades, and blast-glass windows, but it may still succumb to disaster. Preventing potential threats is only useful up to the point of an actual loss, no matter how unlikely. After the loss, the unit is forced to recover. At that time, the unit must rely on the work it has done to prepare.

The focus of prevention is avoiding or minimizing loss. The focus of recoverability is recovering from a loss and returning to an environment in which products and services can be delivered, i.e., a "new normal."

2.1.2 Second Principle: Recoverability Is Not Survivability or Resilience

Second, it is important to posit that recoverability is not survivability or resilience. A common belief is that the purpose of BC is to make an organization more survivable. We find three fundamental problems with this belief.

2.1.2.1 Survivability Offers Too Many Variables

The first problem is the almost innumerable variables that contribute to an organization's survivability, especially looking out years in advance. Listing all the critical components of a successful organization operating under all conceivable circumstances with all the different disciplines that play a role would soon exceed the course listing of every MBA program. Unpacking all the requirements of survivability would far outstrip the proper domain of BC.

2.1.2.2 Survivability Is Too Nebulous

The second problem is that what it means for an organization to "survive" is nebulous. Within the context of a disaster, speakers often focus simply on whether the organization has "survived" the event. But, surely, there are better and worse conditions under which an organization stays in business. Was the organization forced to cut staff, reduce services, and expend capital? Did it lose market share? What are its prospects for the next few years? Or perhaps the business closed its doors but with enough monetary and intellectual capital for the employees to launch a new business that successfully takes advantage of a new market. Neither survivability nor recovery is a yes-or-no proposition.

2.1.2.3 Resilience Is Properly an Inter-Discipline

The purpose of BC is sometimes thought to be to make organizations more resilient. But resilience is actually an *inter-discipline*. While BC may be involved in the pursuit of resilience, the two terms should not be interpreted as having the same meaning. Since an *interdisciplinary* topic generally involves combining two or more academic disciplines or fields of study, it does not represent a discipline in its own right. In this case, resilience might pull from emergency management, risk management, crisis management, psychology, strategic planning, law, and a number of other fields. Thus, it pulls from a set of disciplines in a unique way and therefore warrants its own sphere of study, practice, writing, funding, and subject matter experts. Regardless of which individual disciplines are finally included into the inter-discipline of resilience, BC remains a discipline in its own right and cannot morph or evolve into resilience.

2.1.3 Third Principle: Recoverability Concerns Recovery from a Physical and/or Staffing Loss

Recoverability implies that an organization is preparing to recover from something. But, *from* what is the organization preparing to recover? In this case, we are concerned only with recovering from a *physical* loss or a loss of *staffing*. Thus, recovery preparedness is not prevention, survivability, or resilience, but it is also not issue management or crisis/reputation management. While we will not argue for a particular definition of these terms, in general we understand the following:

- *Issue management* is the lifecycle of monitoring and responding to emerging threats and problems.

- *Crisis/reputation management* is the response to incidents that primarily threaten an organization's brand or reputation.

We do not need to detail the degree of differences; we only need to properly focus the book with this third principle.

2.1.4 Fourth Principle: Recoverability Concerns the Reestablishment of Services, Either Individually or as an Organic Whole

If the term *recoverability* implies that the organization is preparing to recover, then "what" is it recovering? The simple answer is that it is recovering the ability to deliver its products and services. Your organization will likely not look the same as it did before the disaster, but will recover some level, perhaps even an improved level, of services relevant to its core mission. Thus, in many cases, the organization will recover itself to a new level of product and service delivery that can be called "new normal."

Current literature uses many terms to describe this "what" of continuity and recoverability, such as processes, functions, systems, operations, and services. For this book, we use the term *services*. This allows for the inclusion of any process, function, operation, or service that must be resumed to support the core mission of the unit, area, or organization. In many cases the term *services* can also apply to information technology (IT) systems.

It is important to note here that services might need to be recovered individually or as part of an organic whole. Each level of the organization, from the department up to the entire enterprise, has a collection of services that must operate together.

2.1.5 Building a Foundation with the Four Principles

Finally, based on the four principles stated above, a definition and proper scope of recoverability can be formulated:

> **Recoverability:** The ability to restore services, individually and/or holistically, following a physical and/or staffing loss.

The main purpose of the Adaptive BC professional is to continuously improve an organization's ability to recover services, individually and/or holistically, following a physical and/or staffing loss. This mission statement follows directly from the four principles above. Therefore, the core of Adaptive BC must center on recovery *capabilities*. If the BC professional's charge is to improve recovery capabilities, then we must have a solid understanding of what these capabilities are and the potential constraints involved in continuously improving them. We must also have a way to measure these improvements so we know to what degree our Adaptive BC approach is having an effect. We turn now to a model that allows us to establish this foundation.

2.2 The Capability and Constraint Model of Recoverability

In Chapter 1 of this book, we listed seven practices of traditional BC that we argued should be eliminated from your continuity planning work. These seven practices form the core of most BC programs and approaches today. If we eliminate these central activities from continuity planning, what will take their place?

Having delineated the book's subject matter and outlined the use of a few important terms, we can now turn our attention to meatier issues. How can we establish a proper foundation for recoverability and its related activities?

To begin, we need a model that integrates and sets definitive boundaries for BC activities, one that delineates the proper scope for the practice. The capability and constraint model of recoverability we propose is the industry's first theoretical model. While many guides collect disparate activities between two book covers, this is the first model that provides an integrated, academic, and complete framework for the discipline. The rest of this chapter goes into detail to explain this powerful model.

The capability and constraint model of recoverability (which you will see in Figure 2-6) does not dictate a particular order or sequence of activities, so an explanation of the model can begin from any point within the model. That said, since the possibility of unexpected and significant loss is the fundamental driver for an organization to undertake continuity planning, it seems appropriate for us to begin with a discussion of loss.

2.2.1 Types of Loss

Many different risks, threats, and events can cause loss, just as there are many different manifestations of loss. When we focus on recoverability, however, we can limit our discussion to three major types of physical loss: people, things, and locations. No matter what the cause of the loss, the outcome will be the unavailability of a certain number and combination of people, things, and locations.

- *People* are individuals who directly or indirectly support a given process, function, department, product, system, etc.
- *Things* include physical resources as well as electronic and virtual resources.
- *Locations* are the physical environments in which people perform their work using the things they need. They are reserved for space that people and things must occupy in order to support a given service. An argument could be made that locations belongs to the category of things. But we find it helps to think of locations as a separate category. Where *things* define an item of specific makeup and performance, *locations* can vary so long as they provide the space and environmental requirements (water, power, security, temperature, etc.) for the people and things to operate effectively.

Other possible categories of loss, including reputation, future revenue, market share, or intellectual property, are excluded from the purview of recoverability as we have defined it using our four principles above.

One can visualize the degree of loss for any service. In Figure 2-1, the full, outside triangle indicates no loss. Moving in from the corners of the triangle, we increase the amount of loss in the categories of locations, things, and people. The exact size and shape of the inner triangles will depend on the exact amount of loss.

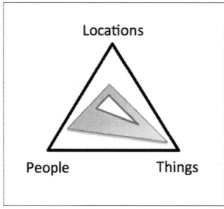

Figure 2-1. Loss Triangle.

Let's take a moment to make a distinction between *actual* and *speculative* loss and to discuss a *range* of loss.

- *Actual* loss constitutes the result of the specific disruption that befalls an organization. It could be measured and graphed as a single, smaller triangle within the larger triangle (not shown here). In this case, the area of the smaller triangle indicates post-disaster availability.

- *Speculative* loss constitutes a potential future loss for which the organization wants to plan. Planners cannot foresee the actual losses that may happen. Therefore, they must work with the organization to determine what kinds of loss to include in their preparedness work.

- For planning purposes, practitioners must work within a *range* of speculative losses. If the potential loss is small enough, there may be no significant interruption to the service and no need for planning. Conversely, if the potential loss is catastrophic enough, the service will simply be unrecoverable and, again, no need for planning.

Therefore, the two smaller triangles within the larger triangle represent the *range* of speculative losses for planning purposes. We will provide specific examples further on in this chapter.

2.2.3 Restrictions

Once a loss has been determined to be significant enough to trigger a response outside of the normal operations of a service, then restrictions come into play. There are three categories of recovery restrictions: time, cost, and scope.

Those familiar with project management may recognize these as the "triple constraint." In the project management discipline, these three constraints represent the restrictions that leadership puts upon the ability to complete any project. Joking aside, leadership does not allow a project to take an unlimited amount of time or spend an unlimited amount of money. Nor are projects allowed to balloon in scope, requiring an ever-growing set of requirements and functionality. In short, the outcome ("quality") of any given project is bounded by limitations in time, cost, and scope.

Likewise, recovery efforts are not allowed to consume unlimited time, cost, and scope. Some services need to be up and running within a strictly defined amount of time. No recovery effort can spend an unlimited amount of money. And there is a degree of functionality that must be restored for a service to provide value.

In Figure 2-2, the restriction triangle, we can visualize restrictions of time, cost, and scope in a manner similar to the loss triangle. The full triangle indicates the regular restrictions applied to normal, everyday operations. Following an incident, these restrictions are likely to *decrease*. More often than not, management must allow more latitude following a disaster by easing up on normal restrictions. Leadership may allow:

- Additional time before resuming services.
- Additional money to purchase the resources it needs to continue services.
- A reduced scope of functionality and/or operations.

Moving in from the outer triangle, the inner triangle represents the decreased amount of restrictions. The exact size and shape of the inner triangle will depend on the exact measures of restrictions. While these are decreased restrictions, they are restrictions nonetheless, and will play a critical role in planning for and recovering from disaster.

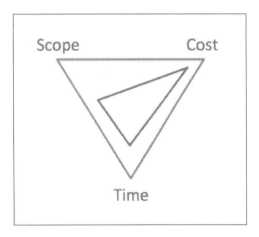

Figure 2-2. Restriction Triangle

Regarding Scope: While it may complicate matters, it is important to note that scope is actually an *inverse* measure. A natural assumption would be that the less time and money you have available for the recovery, the harder it will be. But this is not the case with scope. In fact, reducing the scope of a service that must be recovered actually makes the recovery easier. Thus, a smaller measure of scope must be seen as an inverse restriction.

2.2.4 Loss and Restrictions are Constraints

Taken together, loss and restrictions constitute *constraints* to recoverability. That is, the more loss incurred and the greater the restrictions imposed following a disaster, the harder it will be to recover.

2.2.4.1 Hard and Soft Constraints

Our model considers losses as "hard" constraints. This means they are clear and unmistakable. Specific people are unavailable, certain things are destroyed, and individual floors within a building are inaccessible. There is little ambiguity following a proper assessment of the post-disaster environment. By contrast, restrictions are "soft" constraints. How much are we allowed to spend? How much time can we take? How many functions are important? These restrictions are more subjective because they will vary based on a multitude of factors such as sensitivity to market conditions, branding and reputation, shareholders, and stakeholders, as well as the cultural nuances of the organization and the particular psychology of those involved in recovery. We can combine these loss and restriction constraints as shown in Figure 2-3.

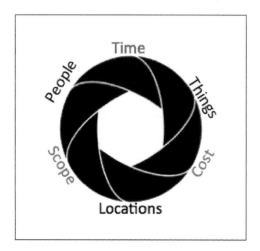

Figure 2-3. Combination of Loss and Restriction Constraints

2.2.4.2 Loss and Restrictions Constrain Both Planning and Recovery

Within the discipline of recovery, the three factors of loss and three factors of restriction combine to set constraints on both planning and recovery efforts.

2.2.4.2.1 Constraints on Planning

For *planning*, the aperture sets the constraints within which the organization will prepare for recovery. Given that we do not plan for zero percent loss, and there is likely no need to plan for 100% loss of people, things, and locations, what are the ranges of loss for which we should plan? And following a loss, what restrictions will leadership place on the time, cost, and scope for recovering each service? It is the job of the professional to help identify and define each of these constraints and establish a consensus among leadership as to the proper level of preparedness desired and effort to be devoted to planning. These are the ranges of constraints. We work within these ranges to improve the organization's recoverability.

2.2.4.2.2 Constraints on Recovery

In an actual *recovery*, the aperture constitutes the constraints within which the organization can recover, coupled with the actual impact of a specific disaster and the actual conditions under which the organization can begin to recover its services at a specific time and place(s). There will be little debate about loss: Following a disaster, loss will be specific and (eventually) apparent. Restrictions, on the other hand, will fluctuate depending on the specifics of the loss and its impact on the organization. These six factors will constrain the organization's ability to recover from disaster, and place specific limits on its ability to exercise its recovery capabilities.

2.2.5 From Constraints to Capabilities

Up to this point, the explanation of the capability and constraint model of recoverability has focused only on constraints. Now it is time to shift focus to capabilities.

Mature organizations spend millions of dollars and countless hours on preparedness. How do they know these efforts are working? To what degree do these efforts improve preparedness? How does a preparedness program demonstrate the progress it has made?

Preparedness can be divided into three capabilities:
1. *Resources* – physical assets required to provide or recover services, such as equipment, hardware, software, locations, staffing, supplies, and vital records.
2. *Procedures* – activities, methods, practices, and instructions for the recovery of services, such as assessment, communication, coordination, mobilization, prioritization, and the reestablishment of services.
3. *Competencies* – characteristics allowing individuals to function throughout recovery, such as fortitude, leadership, shared vision, teamwork, and training.

By way of example, consider the following three brief scenarios:
- A small manufacturing company is without power for many days. While they know how [procedures] to restore each of their production lines, with leaders ready to take charge [competencies] and workers trained for tasks [competencies], there is no other manufacturing equipment available [resources], and they are forced to suspend production.
- A training department loses their building. For the first several days, they suspend all training. But within two weeks, the department staff collaborates across silos [competencies] to identify and obtain teaching space [resources], figure out [competencies] how to make do [procedures] without the usual materials, and then resume most instruction.

- A data center is destroyed by fire, but experienced staff [competencies] utilize a host of predetermined procedures [procedures] to restore services at a fully redundant hot site [resources].

These three components – resources, procedures, and competencies – are *capabilities*. The more of these capabilities available to a service at time of disaster, the more recoverable the service will be. These capabilities can be estimated and compared to what is needed to fully recover at time of disaster. They can be measured over time to track improvements or reductions in recovery capabilities and demonstrate the results of continuity planning efforts.

As presented in Figure 2-4, we can visualize these capabilities in the form of a triangle. The full triangle indicates 100% preparedness. Moving in from the corners of the triangle, we decrease the percentage of preparedness. The area of the smaller triangle therefore indicates actual preparedness.

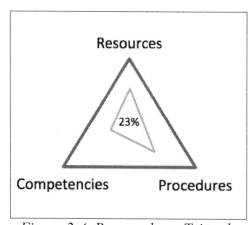

Figure 2-4. Preparedness Triangle

2.2.6 Diving Deeper into Capabilities

This is an important concept so let's dive a little deeper into the nature of each capability.

2.2.6.1 Resources

Resources represent anything the department needs on-hand at time of disaster to provide services and aid in recovery. The list of specific, required resources will vary widely, depending on the nature of any given department, ranging from pencils and paper to plastic molding injectors and nuclear magnetic resonance imaging machines. This is "what" we need to recover. A high-level categorization of resources might be as follows:

- Equipment (including workstations).
- Hardware (firewalls, network switches, physical and virtual servers, etc.).
- Software/applications.
- Space/locations (including HVAC, security, and utilities).
- Staffing.
- Supplies.

- Vital records (including contact information, contracts, documents, and spreadsheets).

2.2.6.2 Procedures

If resources are the "what" of recoverability, then procedures are the "how." These are the strategies and activities that those responsible will use post-disaster in order to continue or restore services. Such procedures will be very different from department to department. The different types of possible procedures may be classified as follows:

- Assess.
- Communicate.
- Coordinate.
- Establish locations.
- Mobilize.
- Prioritize.
- Reestablish services.

2.2.6.3 Competencies

Finally, competencies are the "way" in which we recover. This factor often gets overlooked or is an afterthought in traditional preparedness planning but is every bit as important as resources and procedures. A department or organization that does not have the proper experience, crisis exposure, leadership, and training is going to be far less prepared to recover regardless of the resources and procedures they have. Some writers in the profession have argued that competencies are the only important factors in preparedness and recoverability (Stagl, 2008). Employees must maintain a minimal level of performance while working together to reestablish services, getting out of their day-to-day silos to form effective recovery teams. Individuals must have at least enough fortitude to weather the crisis and assist in recovery. And all must have enough of a shared vision of mission to unite and agree upon what must be done. A high-level classification of competencies might be as follows:

- Crisis fortitude.
- Leadership.
- Performance.
- Shared vision.
- Teamwork.

> **A Word About Strategies and Templates**: There can never be such a thing as a one-size-fits-all template for BC strategies. The profession can, and should, provide a framework and an approach for continuity planning, but it cannot provide specific recovery strategies. Most continuity planners correctly assume cookie-cutter response strategies are not advisable, but many clients request them nonetheless.

To conceptualize the three factors of preparedness, it may be helpful to think of them by way of analogy, as in Table 2-1.

Table 2-1. Capabilities and Analogies

Resources	Procedures	Competencies
"What"	"How"	"Way"
Nouns	Verbs	Adjectives
Stuff	Actions	Characteristics
Things	Activities	Qualities
Availability of physical resources	Knowledge of what to do	Ability to perform throughout a crisis

In a moment, we will combine all this together into a single picture of the capabilities and constraints model, and tie it all together with the concept of an "aperture." Before we can do that, however, we need to talk a little bit about our use of time in preparedness planning. Because time is so important to how we think about and perform our work as BC practitioners, we need to spend a few pages considering time and how we have traditionally misapplied it in our efforts.

2.3 Time: Reframing Our Use of Time

As we mentioned in Chapter 1, it seems impossible to think about preparedness planning without thinking about time. Time is often at the very heart of any discussion of BC. But we've noted that there are deep flaws in the continued attempts to incorporate time into preparedness planning and that these flaws were correctable. As time has been such a central feature in traditional continuity planning, it is important to take the proper space in this chapter to reframe the use of time.

Now that we have encountered the capability and constraint model of recoverability, perhaps we can see the truth about time:

Time is not a target; rather it is a constraint.

Time is neither the only constraint nor even the most relevant. While it has its place in preparedness planning, time does not warrant its central focus in our proposed methodology or practice. Let's take a moment to see why this is the case.

2.3.1 The Restriction Triangle (Revisited)

Previously, we introduced the restriction triangle. We can visualize restrictions of time, cost, and scope as a triangle similar to the triple constraint from project management. The full triangle indicates the regular restrictions applied to normal, everyday operations. Following an incident, these restrictions are likely to *decrease*. More often than not, management must allow more latitude following a disaster by easing up on normal restrictions, by allowing for any of the following:

- Additional time before resuming.

- Additional money to purchase the resources needed to continue.
- A (temporary or permanent) reduced scope of functionality and operations.

Remember that while the outer triangle represents normal, operational restrictions, the inner triangle represents recovery restrictions. These come into play following a disaster. While these are decreased restrictions, they are restrictions nonetheless, and will play a critical role in planning for and recovering from disaster. Thinking about this triangle and the restrictions that the organization will place on our recovery efforts helps us see why time is a constraint, not a target.

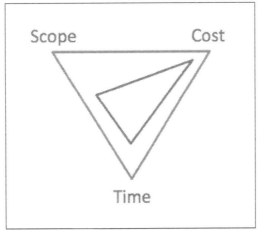

Figure 2-5. Restriction Triangle

2.3.2 Time as a Constraint (Not a Target)

Time in preparedness planning is not a target, then, but one of three constraints. It is the job of the preparedness planner to identify and document all three constraints, not just time. Those in charge of recovery need to know how much money they can spend, how much time they can take, and to what degree of functionality the system or service must be restored. The practitioner should work to define and document these three restrictions, at least at the department level, and preferably at the system or service level.

Some systems and services may indeed have significant recovery time restrictions. The unavailability of a critical service or system might cause:
- Immediate threats to health and safety.
- Violation of laws and/or regulations.
- Failure to meet contractual obligations or service level agreements (SLAs).
- Unacceptable revenue loss.

In these cases, it is essential to understand and document the associated restrictions of time then work to ensure these services or systems can be recovered within the necessary constraints. *These are the only cases for which it is appropriate to set targets of time.*

2.3.3 Time as a Constraint in IT Disaster Recovery

This book is specifically about BC and not IT disaster recovery. But because IT disaster recovery has historically been so intertwined with time, it behooves us to take a moment to touch on the topic. When planning for IT systems, specifically IT disaster recovery for collections of systems or the loss of the entire data center, the key is to determine the proper sequence of recovery. In a personal note to the authors in August 2016, Dan Dorman, IT service continuity manager at Alaska Airlines, explains:

> One of the big issues that illustrates the futility of using time targets is that they can really only apply in a single system failure mode. It may take us 15 minutes to switch a system between data centers in a drill or even in answer to a system failure. But if multiple systems are failing (or the entire data center), other constraints come into play: personnel (with specific skill sets) who cannot recover systems simultaneously, system dependencies, etc. In those situations, it is the systems recovery order that drives the recovery. Recovery efforts are dynamic and attuned to the circumstances of the disaster. Because all disasters differ in the details, we cannot predict the recovery time for multiple systems recoveries, and can only speculate once those details are better known. As a non-bounded judgment, our recovery performance is judged as good, adequate, or below expectations; factored into this judgment is what is and is not in our control.

The proper sequencing for information technology is a matter of interdependencies, not time targets. Infrastructure must be in place before servers; servers must be spun up before databases; databases must be installed before connecting to applications; and so forth. These interdependencies dictate the sequencing. Even systems supporting individual services may have dependencies that dictate the recovery order.

2.3.4 Our New Conception of Time in Adaptive BC

Service owners cannot take all the time they want to recover. Nor can they spend all the money they want. Nor should they necessarily restore all normal functionality when recovering. But given knowledge of established restrictions, along with the potential sequencing of all systems and services, those responsible for recovery are empowered to work autonomously to solve problems, restore services, and get the organization up and running as soon as sensible. Additionally, decision-makers are further empowered to react sensibly to the post-disaster situation as it shifts and unfolds in real time.

The planning process is thereby simplified by eliminating the need to wrangle with participants to set targets of time. Instead of coming to the table with a set of acronyms then pressing for individual time objectives, the planner can be responsive to participants, listening carefully and gathering information in the context in which it is presented. Identifying these restrictions will require the practitioner to interact with all levels of the organization. Such conversations will create a feedback loop: New information discovered during the interactions, the planning process in general, and any actual incidents, may change thinking about practical and actionable levels of restrictions.

The need to capture these three constraints has gone almost completely unrecognized in the discipline. Few practitioners identify what capital will be available at time of disaster specifically to help fund recovery. While insurance may eventually help pay the organization back for some expenditures, departments need to know their options with regard to post-disaster spending. With regard to scope, there is recognition of the need to establish the proper degree of recovery for services in traditional BC practices, as indicated by the increasing use of the hitherto "neglected" minimum BC objective (MBCO) (Maclean-Bristol, 2015). Planners capturing MBCO information collaborate with each service to identify the minimum capacity or functionality needed to recover in order to provide continued value to the organization.

2.3.5 A First Example with Time

Let's consider continuity planning for a hotel. The planning group identifies the following services: accounts payable, accounts receivable, catering, check in/check out, concierge, external phone, internal phone, kitchen, laundry, reservations, and valet. The planner will need to identify and document any restrictions of time, cost, and scope.

In this case, accounts payable must pay its bills within 30 days or incur penalties. This is the only clear restriction of time. Certainly, in a disaster situation, check in/check out services become crucial very quickly, as the hotel needs to know who is staying where in the hotel. Being able to answer and provide information may be critical but no targets of time ought to be associated with these services. They should be restored as soon as sensible based on the extent of the loss and evolving post-disaster situation.

Beyond simply defining time constraints, the practitioner should identify and document scope and cost restrictions. This enables the planning team to establish the degree to which each service should be recovered and any cost restrictions that will come into play during recovery. The identification process will review considerations such as anticipated easing of scope restrictions or spending increases that can be expected in response to a disruptive event in order to get the organization back in business.

2.3.6 Prioritization: Where Did It Go?

It is very tempting, at this juncture, to try and prioritize the recovery order of all services. You might want to argue that, while acceptable to do without specific time targets, the practitioner should still identify the relative business value prioritization of each service. The authors of this book continue to struggle with this temptation as well!

The problem is that the post-disaster recovery prioritization will depend entirely on the actual nature and impact of the disaster on the people, things, and locations at the time the event occurs. As we saw in Chapter 1, the answer to the question of, "How soon does service X need to be up and running?" is almost always, "It depends." Since "It depends" is the most accurate answer, then we cannot prioritize the recovery of all services even while we may need to sequence some recovery activities due to dependencies.

Let's look at our hotel example again. It is tempting to assume that the valet service should be recovered last following an incident; people aren't going to want to stand in line and wait for their car during a disaster. But what if the disaster results in the loss of the hotel's data center? In this case, valet services should continue as normal. If the incident is an ice storm and the guests are stuck at the hotel, then kitchen and laundry services rise to the top, and valet is not offered at all. If the hotel loses power for a long period of time, then check in and check out services are the most important, and the hotel might actually work to provide additional staffing for valet services, bringing it near the top of the recovery list.

In fact, continuing or recovering any individual service is necessary only if its continued existence provides business value to the organization in a post-disaster environment. The organization may decide not to recover a particular service or even an entire department depending on the nature of the disaster. Shortly after Hurricane Katrina, Tulane University was forced to eliminate parts of its medical education program and some graduate teaching positions. The IT department may choose to finally retire a legacy system that has been limping along for many years. The customer base or the market may have shifted significantly, sometimes as a consequence of the disaster.

So not only do time targets disappear, so does prioritization. For those steeped in the tradition of conventional continuity planning, this may be a difficult habit to break. But eliminating this practice will allow practitioners and participants to focus on the core of BC – the continuous improvement of recovery capabilities. The word "adaptive" in Adaptive BC refers not only to the way the practitioner approaches planning in general, but also the way in which the organization approaches recovery.

From here, it becomes more important than ever for those involved in recovery efforts to understand the business of the business. Management and staff cannot rely on a simple list of services prioritized for them beforehand. Those tasked with recovery responsibilities must know the mission of their organization and the objectives of their department. In many cases, these individuals will have to act without direct guidance following a disaster.

Communications are a common challenge in disastrous events. Employees will likely have to act and make decisions on their own, at least for a while. People must be empowered to act, but this is best accomplished if those actions are in line with the vision, mission, values, and objectives of the organization and the employees' departments. For these reasons, we again see why it is so important for the BC practitioner to learn about each department within the organization to improve his or her business acumen.

2.3.7 A Second Example with Time

Let's try another example: continuity planning for a radio station. In this case, the planning group identifies the following services: audience services, emergency broadcast signal, engineering, on-air hosting, operations, promotional content, newsroom, and streaming. The planner needs to identify and document any restrictions of time, cost, and scope.

Let us assume that the only time-based requirement of the station is to transmit an emergency broadcast signal (EBS) once in a 24-hour period. Certainly, in a disaster situation, being able to broadcast and provide news is critically important. But no targets of time ought to be associated with any service other than the EBS. Staff, service owners, and leadership know that many services are absolutely essential to the radio station and need to be recovered as soon as sensible within the realities of a post-disaster situation.

Being able to broadcast the news is dependent upon functioning equipment, so the engineering and operations services must be restored at the outset. On air hosting and the newsroom can be recovered in parallel after operations. Audience services, EBS, streaming, and promotional content can come later. Service restoration owners should be empowered to take action and make decisions to get the radio station back on the air without bottlenecks in communications and approval. Leadership should command at the strategic level, bearing all stakeholders in mind and setting policy to direct the situation as it unfolds.

None of the planning or execution of recovery activities therefore require *targets* of time. Time is a *constraint* specifically in the case of EBS, where the department has 24 hours to broadcast the emergency signal. This is the only time reference that needs to be documented.

Do not forget scope and cost restrictions. These must be identified and documented to enable the planning team to establish the degree to which each service should be recovered and any cost restrictions that will come into play during recovery. If the radio station loses its primary location and equipment, leadership must allow a significant amount of latitude in the quality of broadcasting, something that would never be permitted under normal operations. Leadership will likely also have to identify and provide additional funding to restore services at an alternate location. The continuity planner must work with staff, subject matter experts, and leadership to think through and determine these scope and cost restrictions.

2.3.8 The Elephant in the Room

Participants may still want to know, "How soon will *X* be back up following a disaster?" Leadership may ask this even if it is not brought up in planning discussions. Given the new direction, how does the practitioner answer this question? Answers can include:
1. As discussed in Chapter 1 of this book, it is very likely that establishing credible time targets is a theoretical impossibility. Even if it were theoretically possible,

the costs to the organization to determine (marginally) reliable recovery time estimates make such a determination practically impossible in most cases. One wonders what the estimated recovery time was for Delta's reservation system when it went down for the day on August 8, 2016, what it cost them to obtain that estimate, and what it cost them to assume it was accurate.

2. With specific reference to IT, the practitioner can make a distinction between high availability and disaster recovery. High availability planning may be a good candidate for time targets and recovery estimates. But, as the focus shifts from one end of the loss spectrum to the other, from IT component failures to the loss of entire data centers, time must be excluded. The practitioner must determine the proper sequencing of the interdependences of recovery and the organization's prioritization of individual IT systems without considerations of time.

3. The good news is that time targets are not necessary, nor are prioritization lists. Planning efforts can focus on what is most essential: enabling an organization to continuously increase their capabilities to recover from disaster. The organization can work to measure and continuously improve its recoverability capabilities, oftentimes at the very outset of the planning process. And the preparedness planning effort can deliver measurable value to the organization within days instead of months.

4. Be sure to point out the advantages of this approach, outlined for you in the next section of this chapter.

In short, the practitioner can take the opportunity to change the focus of the discussion as much as possible, warning participants of the limitations with time, and steering the conversation to focus on improving the organization's recoverability capabilities, while taking advantage of the benefits available with the Adaptive BC approach.

2.3.9 Advantages to Eliminating Time Targets

This clearer understanding of the nature of time in preparedness planning solves several traditional problems and offers several new advantages:

- **"It depends" is fully acceptable.** To begin with, the approach solves the problems previously noted with regard to trying to set time targets. "It depends" is now a perfectly acceptable answer from the planning participant. Accepting this answer allows the planning practitioner to be more receptive, adaptive, and effective. The approach enables participants to self-assess restrictions rather than relying on the practitioner to facilitate the assessment of time requirements.

- **It avoids potential conflicts with participants.** In practical terms, the professional avoids potential confrontations with regard to discussions about time. In theoretical terms, the professional does not fall into any traps, as time is discussed only as a constraint to recovery activities, not a target that has to be set without the proper ability to do so. Participants will not feel forced to provide a single, arbitrary answer to meet the needs of a business impact analysis spreadsheet, and the practitioner can maintain a good relationship.

- **It saves money.** Consider a Hotel A that uses a traditional approach and a Hotel B that uses an adaptive approach. Think about the savings when conducting exercises! Hotel A will spend time and effort using exercises to try and validate its ability to hit established recovery time objectives, a dubious venture to begin with. The overriding purpose of such efforts will be to meet predetermined time requirements, and both planners and participants are incentivized to take shortcuts while overlooking or hiding potential problems. Hotel B will use its exercises to try out response strategies, examine its existing capabilities, work on team building and leadership skills, and focus on improving its ability to recover from disaster. The objective, in this case, is to arrive at a realistic understanding of the organization's ability to effectively recover. The incentive is to build capability while looking for opportunities to improve. These improvements alone may warrant the adoption of the Adaptive BC approach we've proposed.

- **It allows for sophistication.** Note that the 24-hour and 30-day time constraints in the prior examples were made intentionally simple for the purpose of this explanation. But this need not be the case. In a personal note to the authors in April 2016, Michael Carpenter points out that there could be several increasingly mature ways to sub-categorize time constraints. The hotel's accounts payable service identified an external 30-day payment restriction, but other drivers could come into play: "There is also the interdepartmental optimization of maximizing interest income from liquid funds available (tactical) and having the proper balance of funds versus investment for liquidity (strategic)." As discussions become more strategic in nature, this approach may help the preparedness professional to engage at higher levels of the organization.

- **It saves time.** Most importantly – and perhaps most shockingly, given current practices – considerations of time virtually disappear along with the time and resource-intensive activities performed in order to establish time-based targets. The result is that practitioners can focus limited resources on increasing the organization's preparedness.

2.4 Putting It All Together: The Aperture of Adaptive BC
2.4.1 What is an *Aperture* (and What Has It Got to Do with BC)?

An aperture is a space or opening. The aperture in a camera controls the amount of light captured on the film or by its digital sensor. In the capability and constraint model of recoverability, the aperture is a window within which something can happen. It sets the boundaries for the focus of all our activities.

2.4.2 High Level Summary of the Capability and Constraint Model

Putting it all together, we can summarize as follows:

- Planning takes place within the limits of anticipated loss and restriction (the aperture).
- The professional's job is to help set the aperture for planning and continuously improve recovery capabilities.
- Actual recovery will happen within the limits of actual post-disaster loss and restriction.
- Time is not a target; it is only one of three constraints.

Thus, the entire model can be combined as shown in Figure 2-6.

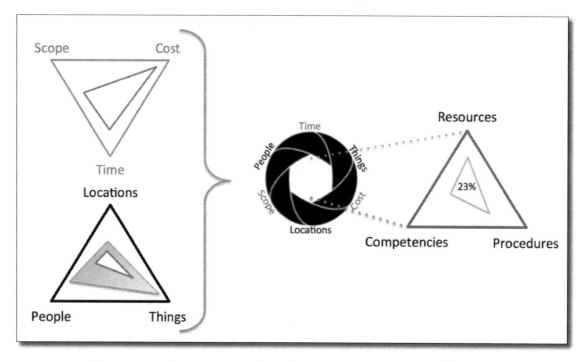

Figure 2-6. The Capability and Constraint Model of Recoverability

In Figure 2-7, you can see the full presentation of the model along with a few helpful labels.

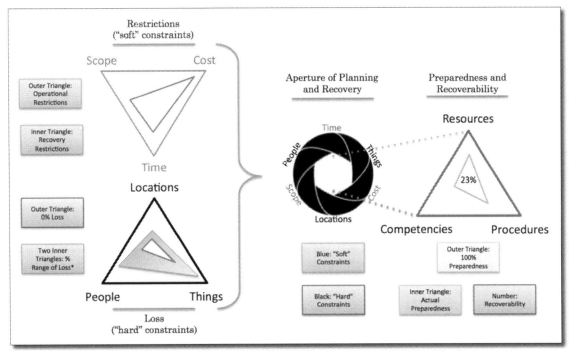

Figure 2-7. The Capability and Constraint Model of Recoverability with Labels.

*Pre-disaster = range of loss for planning purposes; post disaster = actual loss

2.5 One Detailed Example

Before moving on to the next chapter, we thought it might be helpful to provide a full example that takes you through the model, the measurements, and the proper employment of time. This is a very basic, high-level overview of how Adaptive BC would apply and be executed in the real world. More detailed and robust examples utilizing a variety of organizations are provided in Chapter 4.

2.5.1 Our Detailed Example: The G. S. Hotel

Imagine you are the Adaptive BC professional hired to improve the recoverability of the G. S. Hotel. You work directly with Bill Jackson, the general manager. You can start anywhere within the capability and constraint model of recoverability, but Bill and his board of trustees are concerned with being able to recover from loss, so you start with the loss triangle. After a few brief discussions, you determine that the board is most interested in planning for the following loss conditions:

- **33% - 66% loss of staff (people).** The board is concerned about pandemic events. They want to be prepared for an incident that renders a majority of their staff unable to work. If less than one-third of their staff is affected they do not need to plan. (Bill jokes that they just call this "Monday morning.") If more than two-thirds of their staff is unavailable, they will shut everything down. So you only need to plan for a range of loss of people between 33% and 66%.

- **20% - 40% loss of resources (things).** It takes a lot of resources to run a hotel. Up to a 20% loss of things, leadership believes there will be no need to enact a special plan. And they believe that there is no way they would lose more than 40% of their resources without losing the entire hotel, so the upper threshold of loss is set there. This includes IT resources.

- **15% - 75% loss of the hotel (locations).** Regardless of the cause of the disaster, the board wants to improve their ability to recover from a loss of 15% to 75% of the hotel itself. This is their top scenario. If they lose less than 15% of the facilities, they have decided they won't need to enact their plans; if they lose more than 75% of the hotel, they have decided they do not have the capital to recover. Naturally, you work closely with leadership to identify – as clearly as possible – what is, and is not, included within this range.

You are now able to depict these ranges within the loss triangle, as shown in Figure 2-8.

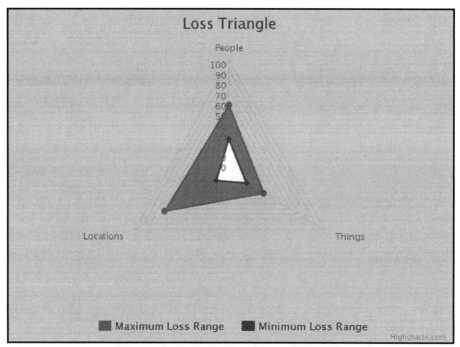

Figure 2-8. G. S. Hotel Loss Triangle

This effort takes less than two hours, and when you show the triangle to Bill and the board they are ready to take the next steps.

Setting the restriction constraints of time, cost, and scope is hard to do for an entire organization and is best done at the department or service level. In addition, you suspect that establishing a baseline measure of preparedness for each department will get you buy-in and support from leadership and other participants. In order to accomplish both, you work with Bill to identify the different departments that comprise the hotel. While we will talk much more about how to accomplish these activities in the next chapter, assume that you meet with each department to identify and understand their services.

After working closely with front-line staff, subject matter experts, managers, and directors for each department, you are able to determine the restrictions in time, cost, and scope for each service. You are also able to do an initial calculation of preparedness, performing a rough measure of available resources, procedures, and competencies (within the established loss parameters, of course). Table 2-2 illustrates what preparedness looks like at a high level.

Table 2-2. Preparedness Baseline for G. S. Hotel

Department	Resources	Procedures	Competencies	Combined
Guest Relations	70%	20%	30%	40%
Guest Registration	25%	60%	95%	60%
Kitchen Services	85%	45%	25%	52%
Administration	70%	100%	45%	72%
Housekeeping	20%	60%	20%	33%
IT	80%	75%	25%	60%
Catering and Banquet	55%	55%	55%	55%
Reservations	15%	77%	60%	52%
Valet	55%	70%	50%	58%
Transportation Services	60%	35%	75%	57%
Gift Shop	50%	90%	75%	72%

Details in Appendix A: You can find more information and a detailed explanation on how to measure preparedness and recoverability in Appendix A.

Putting all the scores together, you get a baseline of organizational preparedness of 53.85%. This means that, at the highest summary level, the G. S. Hotel is roughly halfway prepared to recover from a disaster with the established loss and restriction constraints. This preparedness score can be depicted in the preparedness triangle.

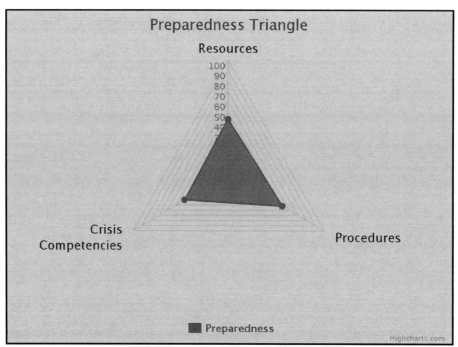

Figure 2-9. G. S. Hotel Preparedness Triangle

You bring these results back to Bill and the board. While they are concerned about the results, they are very pleased with your quick progress, summary information, and visual dashboards.

Given that guest relations is the most important department, you spend some time focusing on that. After talking to the staff and managers of guest relations, you determine that they are only 40% prepared to recover, represented in Figure 2-10.

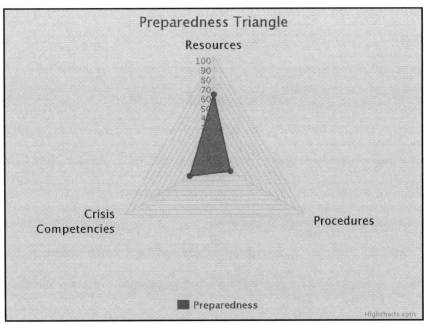

Figure 2-10. Guest Relations Preparedness Triangle

You also talk about housekeeping because it is only 33% prepared to recover.

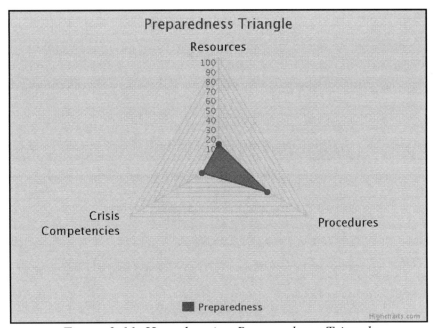

Figure 2-11. Housekeeping Preparedness Triangle

Naturally, Bill and the board ask what makes the housekeeping scores so low. In reviewing the detailed results you point out that while the housekeeping folks knew they would be granted some additional time to turn over rooms, they assumed there would be no special recovery budget available to them. Housekeeping's restrictions triangle is shown in Figure 2-12.

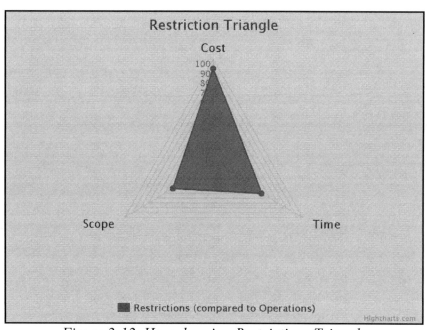

Figure 2-12. Housekeeping Restrictions Triangle

You inform Bill and the board that if a budget of $7,500 dollars a week were made available following a disaster, then this would allow the housekeeping folks to obtain a temporary washer and dryer to launder sheets and towels. Leadership agrees, and within two weeks you have a contract in hand and the housekeeping staff has met to discuss and exercise. Having reduced the restrictions and improved resources and competencies in particular, housekeeping's new preparedness score is 57%, an improvement of 24% in just two weeks!

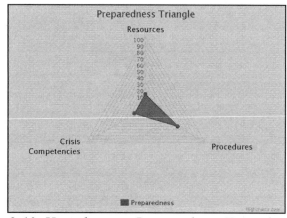

Figure 2-13. Housekeeping Preparedness Triangle (before)

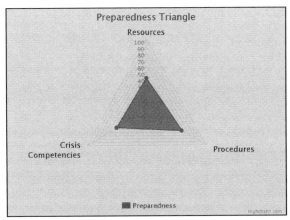

Figure 2-14. Housekeeping Preparedness Triangle (after)

At this point, you meet briefly with Bill and the board to discuss next steps. Using the preparedness baseline as your guide, you identify the biggest gaps and begin the process of continuously improving recovery capabilities. After six months you reset the aperture (there are just a few adjustments to make) and take another preparedness baseline. You demonstrate an improvement of 31% across the entire organization! After spending your big bonus, you settle in for the next six months of work.

2.5.2 Traditional BC Activities You Eliminated (In Our Example)

Let us quickly remind you of the activities you did *not* do:

- **You didn't do a business impact analysis.** Working with Bill and the board, you quickly determined the relative value of each department. You worked with each department to identify and categorize their services. You saved time, money, and relationship capital by moving on.
- **You didn't do a risk assessment.** You didn't need to guess at the cause of any disaster; instead, you worked with Bill and the board to identify the loss parameters for locations, people, and things.
- **You didn't set recovery time targets.** You saved significant effort as well as the emotional capital you might have exhausted trying to nail these down for every service. Instead, you identified the few instances in which time was an important restriction while making strong gains by adjusting constraints of cost and scope.
- **You didn't test.** You used exercises to try out new procedures and equipment, gaining important information instead of trying to validate recovery time objectives through testing. You identified existing capabilities and set targets for improvement.
- **You didn't have to sell executives on every aspect of your approach up front.** You didn't need special permission from Bill and the board to do the work they hired you to do. You didn't take hours of their valuable time explaining the intricacies of BC and the jargon of our profession. You provided them with actionable information when they needed it.

- **You didn't waste time.** You delivered significant value in quick iterations. Because you set the aperture and measured preparedness capabilities, you were able to target the low-hanging fruit and deliver quick wins. In short order, you set about improving capabilities and were able to quantifiably demonstrate significant progress over the first six months.

So how, exactly, did you so quickly and significantly improve capabilities in those first six months? You used the approach outlined in Chapter 3.

References

Amundsen, C. (2014). *Business continuity management and perceptions of impact: An exploratory study of perceptions among professionals and practitioners within the field* (Master's dissertation, The University of Winchester (UK), Winchester Business School).

Maclean-Bristol, C. (2015, November 5). *The minimum business continuity objective: The Cinderella of the BIA...* Retrieved from http://www.continuitycentral.com/index.php/news/business-continuity-news/640-the-minimum-business-continuity-objective

Stagl, J. (2008). DRII, ASIS, NFPA? They're all missing the point. *Continuity Insights, 6*(5), 20.

Chapter 3

Framework

In Chapter 1, we showed you the many failings and problems within traditional business continuity, and identified practices that should be eliminated. In Chapter 2, we presented the capabilities and constraints model of recoverability and how it provides a full foundation for business continuity (BC) planning. While Chapter 1 told you what *not* to do, and Chapter 2 provided the foundation for your planning efforts, this chapter explains the concepts and elements of the Adaptive Business Continuity (Adaptive BC) approach.

This is the nuts and bolts of how to execute Adaptive BC. We will start with an explanation of what Adaptive BC is and talk about the Adaptive BC Manifesto. Next, we will walk you through common steps involved in the approach. Be forewarned: The Adaptive BC approach is neither linear nor sequential, so it helps to be adaptive!

In Chapter 4 we will provide several narratives to illustrate what our framework might look like in practice, and in Chapter 5 we will cover some important considerations and consequences of Adaptive BC and what it means for the future of the discipline.

This chapter will help you to:
- Define and describe Adaptive BC.
- Understand the Adaptive BC Manifesto and why it is important.
- Learn the steps to implementing Adaptive BC.
- Start to guide your program using the Adaptive BC framework.

3.1 What Is Adaptive Business Continuity?

Adaptive Business Continuity is a flexible and outcome-oriented alternative to traditional continuity planning. Its focus is the continuous improvement of an organization's capabilities to recover from disruption and disaster.

Adaptive BC draws from the far-reaching management trends (some of which are discussed in Chapter 5) that have developed in project management and process improvement, including:

- *Agile project management*, which emphasizes responding to unpredictability through flexible work processes and feedback.
- *Lean process improvement*, which defines value and organizes to deliver what is needed when it is needed, as reflected in work processes and feedback.

Adaptive BC uses these trends to facilitate the rapid enhancement of recovery capabilities. The practitioner should work in short cycles to prioritize efforts and produce deliverables that provide value to the organization. Adhering to the principles of the Adaptive BC Manifesto, practitioners should develop their business acumen, taking time to learn about the mission and culture of the organization, and adapting to the needs of each department, instead of forcing a strict methodology across all parts of the organization.

The Adaptive BC approach is nonlinear, allowing the practitioner to prioritize efforts based on the relative value provided. Throughout the process, the planner adapts to the needs and culture of each department, improving existing capabilities and empowering employees to adapt to disruptive events as they unfold. Planning is social and collaborative, requiring the practitioner to work and build trust with all participants. The required outcomes of the BC program should be balanced with the environment of the organization.

3.1.1 Resources, Procedures, and Competencies

As detailed in Chapter 2, an organization's recovery capabilities consist of resources, procedures, and competencies. Each of these can be measured by assessing what the organization needs for recovery compared to what is already shown to be in place. Within the discipline of BC, the three factors of loss and three factors of restriction combine to set constraints on planning and recovery efforts.

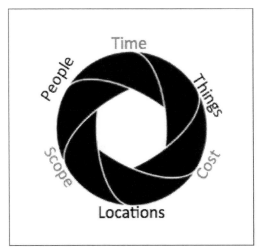

Figure 3-1. Aperture of Planning and Recovery

All planning takes place within an *aperture* of constraints, namely loss and restriction, as explained in Chapter 2:

- **The constraints of loss: things, people, and locations.** Regardless of what causes a disaster, these three categories of loss will be affected. The practitioner must identify the range of loss for which each department will plan. Following an incident, the actual loss will constrain actual recovery efforts.
- **The constraints of restrictions: time, cost, and scope.** The practitioner must help determine how much latitude each department will have in these three categories when they have to recover.

The practitioner will continuously improve competencies while refining the aperture of loss and restrictions.

Every step in the Adaptive BC process should be plain and transparent to leadership and participants.

- Establish clear expectations and demonstrate progress using rapid cycles of delivery.
- Provide leadership and stakeholders with flexible options for the next set of deliverables.

With a clear view of the work and approval of rapidly produced deliverables, buy-in should improve alongside the recovery capabilities.

3.2 The Adaptive BC Manifesto

In the Introduction to this book, we presented a summary of the Adaptive BC Manifesto along with a little bit of the history behind it. The manifesto is a distillation of our thinking about the BC industry and how Adaptive BC can improve the efforts of its practitioners. We encourage you to read the full Adaptive BC Manifesto in Appendix B of this book right now!

3.2.2 Principles Are Not Deliverables

Recall that there are nine principles in the manifesto. Note that we call these "principles." This means they are not specific deliverables or actions. To the extent possible, all nine principles should apply to any activity being performed. When exercising for improvement, for example, the practitioner may use the exercise as an opportunity to measure and benchmark while learning the business and engaging new participants. Exercise activities can even be used to reinforce the use of documents as mnemonics while preparing for effects and not causes.

Traditional BC emphasizes the creation of tangible products, usually documents, to satisfy sequential steps in the process. To date, there has been little concern or guidance as to how to evaluate the quality of those deliverables or the value they produce. Traditional BC emphasizes the execution of specific activities instead of focusing on the end goal of improving an organization's recovery capabilities. Many times this is done primarily to meet "check-the-box" requirements for regulators and auditors. In contrast, Adaptive BC seeks to weave all the necessary aspects of effective recoverability into a holistic, integrated approach. This is one important way the Adaptive BC approach enables practitioners to deliver continuous value in short iterations, a feat that is difficult to achieve following traditional practices.

3.3 How Do I Execute Adaptive Business Continuity?

Let us begin with an analogy. Suppose you go to the doctor and he or she tells you that you need to improve your health. Specifically, you need to eat better and exercise more. Imagine, then, that the doctor gives you a list of exactly what to eat at each of three meals for the next six weeks along with a complete exercise regimen to be performed at 5:17am, 12:04pm, and 7:52pm each day. This might strike you as unusual, if not downright presumptuous! While some general guidance is helpful, such as types of nutritious food and exercise, it would be counterproductive for the doctor to assign you a meal-by-meal regimen.

3.3.1 The Role of the BC Professional

This brief analogy helps us better understand the proper role of the BC professional and the limits of what we can recommend as it relates to the Adaptive BC approach. Think of your role as a BC professional in relation to the rest of the organization as being like that of a medical practice in relation to the patients:

- You can find numerous ways to improve recovery capabilities as you can find numerous ways to improve your health.
- A proper BC approach should not focus on a detailed list of deliverables just as an unfamiliar doctor should not provide you with a specific meal plan and exercise regimen.
- Continuity planning is not a one-size-fits-all endeavor and neither is maintaining your health, though general and helpful recommendations exist for both.

- The BC practitioner must learn about the business and try for quick wins just like a specialist learns about you and tries for fast results.
- There must be as much of a fit as possible among the BC practitioner, the practice, and the organization, just as there must be as much fit as possible among the health specialist, the practice, and the client.
- There are ways to measure improvements in recovery capabilities just as there are ways to measure improvements in general health.

The most important point to keep in mind is that the job of the practitioner is the continuous improvement of recovery capabilities. That must always be the foundation for the work and the end goal of the program. How does the Adaptive BC professional do this? The simple answer is to use the foundation outlined in Chapter 2:

- Set and refine the aperture.
- Assess and improve capabilities (within the aperture).

To the extent that you are improving capabilities within the spirit of the manifesto, you are executing Adaptive BC! Results should not be evaluated using a checklist of physical deliverables. The proper outcomes of the Adaptive BC approach are improved capabilities. We are not interested in producing documents and spreadsheets. Instead, we demonstrate our value by measuring the improvements in recovery capabilities.

3.3.2 Activities Within the Adaptive BC Framework

We understand that some practical guidance will be helpful as you start down the Adaptive BC path. In what follows, we will outline concepts and common activities to execute Adaptive BC while leaving the door open for a great deal of flexibility. You do not need to execute any items in any of these sections in any particular order. You can begin with any step that makes the most sense to you within the culture and mission of the organization and its individual departments. In Chapter 4, we will look at different scenarios and provide specific guidance as to what actions might make the most sense given certain environments and cultures. The remainder of this chapter is divided into three major sections to get you started and provide some guidance:

- Set direction (and the aperture, as shown in Figure 3-1).
  - Set program direction.
  - Set departmental level direction (including loss constraints).
  - Identify services (including restriction constraints).
  - Kickoff/re-group.
  - Set iterations.
- Improve capabilities.
  - Assess capabilities.
  - Exercise capabilities.
  - Address ad hoc opportunities.
  - Improve capabilities.

- ○ Improve your customized response portfolios.
- Refine.

3.3.3 Set Direction

You are going to have to communicate with people to explain who you are, what you hope to accomplish, and how you will approach the work. Such discussions are the topic of this section on setting direction. Whether it's your first meeting with the board, your second meeting with a vice president, or your tenth meeting with a work group, you are likely going to have to provide current status, updates, information, and next steps. As these activities are common to any new endeavor and because they can get you off to a bad start if not performed properly, we begin our discussion with them.

3.3.3.1 Set Program Direction

Imagine you have been hired to launch a BC program within an organization. You did not sneak in and start BC planning covertly. You were brought in by someone to take on the task of building a BC Program. During the hiring or onboarding process, you likely gained valuable information about what was expected from you and the BC program. This information alone might be enough to get you started!

When you started in the organization, it is likely that someone gave you information about where to begin, what leadership expects, how to set your first meeting, when to report status, and the like. If so, then feel free to skip to a different step in our list. If you need more information about the strategic direction for your Adaptive BC program, work with leadership to learn, at a minimum, the answers to these questions:

- Are there specific deliverables that leadership wants you to produce?
- Does leadership expect these deliverables in a certain amount of time?
- Does leadership have a vision of what a successful BC program looks like?
- Is leadership concerned about specific loss scenarios? (Set your aperture!)
- Is there a deadline for completion of program deliverables with designated departments?
- Is there a protocol for scheduling and conducting meetings with each department?
- What advice can leadership offer about how best to position your program for success?
- Which department(s) should be in the first phase of BC planning efforts?

Obtaining this information might take minutes or hours. It is possible you will be able to engage with individual senior leaders, develop trust, and convert them into champions for your work. Stakeholders may want to talk to you about BC for hours on end. But it is just as likely that getting time with senior leadership is difficult or impossible. Either way, you can still be effective and make progress. Learn what you can about their expectations as well as the business of the organization. Remember that you only need enough information to get started with your planning efforts. Anything more is a bonus!

From time to time, you may be able to check in with leaders individually or as part of a committee. This is your opportunity to obtain incremental direction from them and deliver continuous value. Use these forums to showcase your progress. Highlight important deliverables. Show them the capability baseline along with shortcomings in preparedness and recoverability. Refine the aperture based on what you learn and get ready for the next phase of your work: to improve capabilities.

Keep in mind the principles from the manifesto. This early stage of the process provides ample opportunity to learn the business and engage at many levels within the organization. As a practitioner, you might even manage to get some early measurements and benchmarks, while getting leadership to stop worrying about the myriad of threats and focus on loss effects instead. If you are a stakeholder or executive, use this time to educate the practitioner on your goals and objectives for the program. Educate him or her about your business and what is valuable to your executive team. Learn what you need to know about the BC program, and provide enough information and authority to get it on its way. This will help you avoid the pitfalls outlined in Chapter 1, follow a sound methodology from Chapter 2, and align with the principles of the manifesto.

3.3.3.2 Set Department Level Direction
It is possible you may never talk to anyone in the C-suite your entire career. The executive who authorized the program might never think of it or you again. Despite what traditional continuity planners might say, this is a perfectly common and acceptable situation. This may seem surprising, but recall that we are talking specifically about BC and not related disciplines like emergency management or crisis management. BC is neither strategic planning nor management consulting. Adaptive BC focuses on the continuous improvement of recovery capabilities. As long as the process can continue, engaging directly with senior leadership is an advantage, not a requirement.

We assume, for the remainder of this chapter, that the BC practitioner will partner with individual managers to improve recoverability capabilities at the *department* level. This does not have to be the case – circumstances may dictate that the BC program focuses at higher or lower levels than a department. For the sake of simplicity, we will assume your organization will be planning with any number of specific departments.

In departmental direction-setting, the practitioner works with stakeholders to determine a high-level scope of work. A stakeholder could be a vice president, department director, manager, subject matter expert, executive assistant, or any collection of people assigned from the department to "make this continuity thing happen." You do not have to explain everything about BC or your program. You just need enough buy-in to execute your work. If stakeholders are interested and willing to learn more about BC, consider it a bonus and work to build additional trust and rapport.

Here are some things you should learn from stakeholders in order to establish a footing for first steps:

- Are there any specific deliverables or timeframes you have in mind?
- Do you have any specific disaster-related concerns or "hot button" issues?
- What should I know about your department and business?
- With whom should I start working?
- When would you like me to check in with you again?

Spend more time listening instead of presenting. In the end, you only need to get permission to work with a knowledgeable person(s) to take the next step in planning. Do not use jargon or dictate all the steps you will make the group take in the future. If there is time and interest, you might want to discuss the following:

- The general advantages of undertaking BC planning.
- The Adaptive BC approach.
- What you plan on delivering first.
- Your next steps.

3.3.3.2.1 Clearing Roadblocks to Execution

Many, many practitioners report having trouble obtaining the permissions and information they need to get started. For that reason, we would like to provide a few suggestions for negotiating potential obstacles in departmental direction-setting. If you hit a roadblock, remember to learn what is important to your stakeholders, then use their vocabulary. Speak in terms of strategic value and what is important to them. You can stress the very true facts that:

- They know their business better than you do.
- Their help is important to your success.
- You do not want to waste anyone's valuable time.
- Your mission is to further protect them by improving their recovery capabilities.

You may find that lack of a response or limited time on the calendar with a department's leader is preventing you from making meaningful progress. While such a situation is not desirable, it is not insurmountable. Be adaptive and learn to engage with other people. You may have to obtain an organizational chart or work with the executive assistant to identify managers, supervisors, subject matter experts, and other key players in the department. Have a brief chat with each of them. This will provide you the opportunity to learn the business as well as determine who is most helpful and engaged. Some of them may well become your champions further down the road. Continue to engage with the individuals who have the most interest in what you are doing and provide the most benefit to your success. You might be able to get leaders from different departments to talk to this individual and convince him or her of the value you provide. Perhaps you can bring some positive peer pressure to bear. This is how we engage at many levels of the organization!

Being adaptive sometimes means clearing a path and not always following the beaten one. The important step is to make progress even if your initial steps are small. When time becomes available on the manager's calendar you'll already have accomplishments to share. This goes a long way in establishing credibility and demonstrating an ability to provide value.

Make sure to set and refine the aperture. At a minimum you need to establish the ranges of loss constraints for people, things, and locations, as you will need this for your planning. You may also be able to identify some restrictions of time, cost, and scope, though you will likely not be able to identify most of these restrictions until you identify services.

3.3.3.3 Identify Services

As you partner with the members of each new department, you need to figure out what they do and how they think of their work. Remember, a "service" is just a way to encapsulate the various processes, functions, products, offerings, and benefits that a department provides. Providing services is the reason a department exists, and services are what the BC practitioner is dedicated to protect and recover.

Work with participants to determine what they do in their department and then create a list of services. For some folks, it may be the first time they have ever had to categorize the work in their department in this way, so be sure to guide them through this process. Your list should capture, at a high level, all the work that the department does.

While you could target and make capability improvements at the departmental or even organizational level, in most cases the proper focus is on services. We focus on improving recovery capabilities for services precisely because everyone will judge our recovery efforts by our ability to restore services. You might think of services as the atoms of all planning activities, with the three types of capabilities forming the protons, neutrons, and electrons of that atom. By improving capabilities, we strengthen the services that make up a department.

What is the right level of specificity for this list of services? Ideally, this list would serve as both an at-a-glance reminder for folks to reference when they want to think about the whole of their department's offerings and as a prompt for post-disaster assessment, mobilization, direction, and reporting. Your list should not be too short or high-level as to render service-specific preparedness activities meaningless. Nor should it be too specific so as to mire your planners in too much detail. This is not a business process reengineering activity where you create a workflow for every process and handoff within and between departments. We just want to get a good feel for what services would be lost if resources used by this department were suddenly unavailable.

3.3.3.3.1 Setting the Aperture (with Restriction Constraints)

Once you have identified the department's services, set the aperture. Apply the loss constraints and identify the restriction constraints. Begin by informing or reminding participants of the range of loss constraints set for your planning work. If it makes sense to do so, explain the three types of loss, namely things, people, and locations, and make sure that everyone involved understands the range of anticipated loss for which you are planning. Talk about and identify the restrictions of time, cost, and scope; help them understand that normal restrictions will almost always be relaxed in a post-disaster environment. Take the time to determine and document specific restrictions for each service as we covered in Chapter 2:

- **Time:** Are there any specific restrictions on the time needed to reestablish this service due to regulations, penalties, safety, legal, contractual obligations or other drivers?
- **Cost:** Will additional money be provided following a disaster, if needed to help reestablish this service?
- **Scope:** Given the range of loss for which we are planning, what is the minimal functionality you need to reestablish for this service to be effective?

It may take participants a little time to think their way through these considerations, particularly when discerning the proper scope for the recovery of each service. Give them the time they need and help them through the process. As we learned in previous chapters, because we do not have to establish any time targets, participants are free to talk about recovering different levels of functionality. It is perfectly acceptable to document scope restrictions in terms of functionality over time if that helps you, your participants, and those charged with recovery. Be sure to take the trouble to document the post-disaster scope for each service, for while it takes a little extra effort, it will be very important to future planning and recovery efforts. You can further refine these scope descriptions at any time, as you all will continue to learn as you move through planning iterations.

3.3.3.3.2 Avoiding the Prioritization of Services for Recovery

It will be tempting, particularly for experienced BC planners, to prioritize services by importance or criticality. But remember that, depending on the type and impact of the disaster, these priorities may change drastically. Trying to define a sequence for recovery of services may inhibit the flexibility needed to respond effectively. Therefore, resist the temptation to put the list in priority order. We recommend you put the list in alphabetical order by service name to reinforce the fact that recovery sequence may be fully dependent upon the post-disaster situation. If it is more helpful to your participants and stakeholders to see the list in some other order, that is fine.

Remember to work in accord with all the Adaptive BC principles from the manifesto. You are already learning the business and, hopefully, engaging with many levels within the organization. This is an ideal time to remind your participants that they are preparing for effects and not causes. Do not create a binder of documentation; you can probably capture all the results of this step on a single sheet of paper to be used in both planning and recovery efforts. Remember that you are not aiming to deliver a document, but rather the continuous improvement of recovery capabilities.

3.3.3.4 Kickoff

You may find value in marking the beginning of your work with some sort of kickoff activity. This might be a meeting where you, as the BC executive or planner, formally present BC and the value you hope to deliver. It might be a five-minute phone call to bring a new participant up to speed. It might even be a fancy catered lunch for a whole department (but we doubt it). Regardless of how you mark the occasion, this is your opportunity to set the stage for your relationship with the folks who will be participating in your effort.

A kickoff usually occurs the first time you are meeting with participants. At a minimum, you want to give participants an idea of who you are, why the work you all are doing is important, and what they can expect in the immediate future. Depending on how much time you have and what makes sense for the individuals in this specific department, consider addressing some of the following topics:

- How business continuity differs from emergency management, IT disaster recovery, crisis management, and other related disciplines.
- How long this might take based on your past experience.
- How much time might be needed from each of them.
- How they will be involved in setting next steps and contributing to the work.
- What BC is, in general.
- What Adaptive BC is, specifically.
- What losses you should prepare for (the loss settings of your aperture).
- What participants can expect as you work together.
- What you hope to achieve with them.

In turn, you are encouraged to learn some things from them. Depending on how much time you have and what makes sense in the context of this specific department, here are some questions you might consider:

- Are there any specific disaster scenarios about which you are worried?
- Are there any specific disaster-related worries or concerns you have?
- Do you have any questions about BC?
- Do you have any questions about disasters?
- Has anyone been through a disaster situation and what was their experience?
- Is there anything specifically you would like me to know about your department?
- Would this group like to talk at some point about how to prepare families and households for disaster?

A Word About Life Safety: Be sure to help participants understand the critical difference between business continuity and emergency management. Unless you are responsible for both disciplines, you must inform participants that while it is critically important that they plan for employee health and safety after an event, your job is to plan for continuity of their services.

Practitioners have many ways to run a kickoff session, and we will not try to cover them all here. But keep in mind the nine principles of the manifesto as well as the other tools in your arsenal as you run these sessions. You could try running a tabletop exercise as part of your initial discussion. You could take a quick preparedness baseline to help them understand right away where improvements can be made. Bottom line: Think about the value you can provide as part of a kickoff.

Remember, this does not have to be a formal or even a one-time event. This could be the first step in obtaining incremental direction from leadership. As you meet with different participants throughout each department, they may not have any idea of who you are or what you are doing. You may wish to develop several different "flavors" of kickoff presentations, ranging from a two-minute summary to a 15-minute overview. Each time, be sure to build rapport with your participants and learn as much as you can about them and their business. A key insight from a frontline worker might just be the information that proves most valuable in the days to come!

Make It Memorable: While our profession does not often talk much about the critical importance of soft skills, here is one of many cases where they show their value. In your work for the kickoff or re-group outcome, make sure to put yourself in the best light possible. Avoid the temptation to present yourself as a "master of disaster" who speaks in industry jargon, pushes an inflexible agenda, and emphasizes the worst-case scenario. Instead, position yourself as a business professional who is working to further protect each department while learning about its mission, services, culture, and people.

3.3.3.4.1 Re-Grouping

A re-group step is needed when there is a change in the expected direction of work with a department. In other words, you may need to do a re-group step when something has happened to interrupt the regular flow of the work process and iterations you had anticipated. The likely causes of such interruptions and changes include:

- Change in leadership.
- Change in mission or function.
- Merger or acquisition.
- New product or service offering.
- New technology.
- Organizational restructuring.
- Turnover in key staff.

Being an Adaptive BC professional, such changes are not a worry for you or your program. Changes in direction are inevitable, and adapting with such changes will position you as a team player. Anticipate and welcome them!

Do not confuse the departmental direction-setting outcome with the kickoff/re-group outcome. The first concerns figuring out what should be done while the second concerns informing participants about what they can expect. The first involves learning about expectations from stakeholders, while the second involves learning about the participants themselves and their department. They both concern building a relationship of trust and improving your business acumen. Both can even take place in the same meeting.

In keeping with the spirit of Adaptive BC, you continuously improve each department's capabilities to recover from disaster by producing valuable deliverables in rapid succession. With the kickoff/re-group activity, you may feel that you are not directly contributing to this continuous improvement mission, but you are improving capabilities merely by expanding employees' awareness of BC, risk, and disaster preparedness.

3.3.3.5 Set Iterations

Before we conclude our discussion on setting direction, note that all direction setting is an iterative and ongoing process. The customer does not have to know everything about your program and you do not have to identify all deliverables up front. It is enough to know the general direction, partner with participants, and work to identify and produce each set of deliverables as efficiently as possible. But you should frequently involve your stakeholders and workgroups in setting the next steps of your work. This means that you might spend a few minutes of every meeting with executives, leaders, and participants talking about what you delivered recently, what you learned from that iteration of work, and what you propose to do next. Ensure that stakeholders are as involved as possible in determining the next outcome and general direction of your work together.

You can set iterations in many ways. You can remind folks of the specific goals that you have worked together to identify, how much progress you have made, and what is left to do. Based on how long it has taken to complete improvement initiatives to date, you can estimate how long it will take to finish off the current set of targeted deliverables. If you are a project manager by trade, you will be tracking the work of your BC program and providing updates at the end of every meeting with stakeholders. You might simply use a handful of sticky notes to show participants where you are in the process of performing the BC work for them, and have them place the remaining sticky notes in the order that they want the rest of the work to get done. You might even consider taking each step outlined in this chapter of the book, writing it down on a sticky note, and letting your departmental participants chose the order in which you all want to perform each step. Be sure to always involve your stakeholders in the direction setting process, and use it to deliver value in rapid delivery cycles.

3.3.4 Improve Capabilities

Improvement activities constitute anything you and your departments do to improve recovery capabilities. That is a pretty broad spectrum! It encompasses all the ways you could improve resources, procedures, and competencies. As you would expect, we cannot describe the many ways you could go about doing this, just as we cannot list all the ways you can improve your health. But we do want to try and offer some suggestions to get you started.

Improved recoverability is the ultimate goal of planning and preparedness efforts. As such, the practitioner partners with individual departments across the organization to improve capabilities. Measuring resources, procedures, and competencies allows departments to better understand where they stand in their existing ability to recover from disaster. In this regard, no service has to start from scratch in preparedness efforts; every service has some capabilities for recovery, and can work to improve those capabilities over time. A baseline allows both the department and the practitioner to demonstrate the improvements and the value that preparedness efforts bring to the organization over time.

We have identified five broad activities in this category, and we will discuss each one below:

- Assess capabilities.
- Exercise capabilities.
- Address ad hoc opportunities.
- Directly improve capabilities.
- Improve your customized response portfolio.

3.3.4.1 Assess Capabilities

Are your efforts producing value? Is your BC program actually improving your organization's ability to recover from disaster? How better prepared is each department after you work with them? These types of questions are almost impossible to answer with traditional continuity planning, but lie at the heart of the Adaptive BC approach. As we continue to offer suggestions for how to execute Adaptive BC work, we now turn to assessment. With assessment, we work to determine existing recovery capabilities and set a baseline against which to measure improvements.

This is probably where Adaptive BC varies most drastically from traditional approaches. As we have discussed previously, the common approach to measurement is to count deliverables and materials or to track the time that has elapsed since specific BC activities were last completed. While a list of pending activities drives action to produce deliverables, it lacks what is most needed: an objective assessment of how prepared the organization is to effectively respond and recover from significant disasters and disruptions.

Measures and baselines are a critical component of the Adaptive BC approach. After all, as the saying goes, what gets measured gets done. When it comes time to improve the organization's recoverability, it helps to know what needs the most attention. It also helps to know if your changes are having the intended outcome after the fact. Measures provide good information to share when meeting with leadership and management. Baselines provide targets and objectives for your improvement efforts, as well as potential motivation for participants. We are often surprised at how receptive participants can be when challenged to meet specific, measurable improvement goals.

3.3.4.1.1 Owning Metrics

Before we proceed, we should cover one important concept in Adaptive BC as it pertains to measurement, namely getting more people to "own" the measurements. Under traditional approaches to BC planning, metrics are the domain of the BC planner and program. It is BC practice that determines what should be counted and BC planners who serve as the custodians of that data. The BC practitioners evaluate the success and effectiveness of the BC program itself primarily by checking the box associated with their next allotted task. Adaptive BC seeks to change this paradigm by tasking many different people with evaluating the preparedness of the organization. This means BC practitioners are no longer the sole evaluators of program quality. Nor are they the only keepers of data. This may be a scary prospect as it takes evaluation responsibility out of the hands of the "experts." But, as we have already said, BC professionals are not the authorities on the businesses they support and should not be the primary determiners of the value of program deliverables. If the work being provided is not useful to the business, then it is wasted effort.

Let's first look at the two types of measurements available to us specifically within Adaptive BC. After that we will provide various methods for collecting the data for these measurements.

3.3.4.1.2 Measuring Resources, Procedures, and Competencies

The first type of measurement evaluates the availability and usefulness of existing capabilities: resources, procedures, and competencies needed to effectively respond to and recover from serious disruption. The value of this approach is:

- It paints a clear picture of the organization's state of recoverability.
- It provides details around what steps the department should take to improve its overall recovery capabilities. If available resources are low but procedures and competencies are relatively high, then it becomes clear where to invest for the purpose of improving overall recoverability.
- It shows leadership and participants that they are not starting from scratch, and that you will work together to build on capabilities that already exist. In this way, you are already working within the culture and mission of each individual department.

- It provides an ideal forum for the practitioner to learn the business.

Setting and refining loss and restriction constraints, as outlined in Chapter 2, is also a measurement. This can be an initial discussion or query about existing restrictions as well as anticipated losses in a post-disaster environment. Or it can be a review of the current state with the intention of building consensus or refining existing restrictions. Either way, a clearer picture emerges that is then understood and shared by all. As others weigh in, the organization establishes consistency in its measures and opportunities for correction. These measures inform the planning process by establishing parameters but also inform leaders and participants about expectations. This avoids the common pitfall of unrealistic expectations when disaster happens.

How do we obtain the data we seek? One of the most effective means is through surveys. Surveys are effective because they are relatively easy to distribute and very scalable. Once a survey is developed it can be distributed to an increasing number of individuals to expand the volume of data collected and, hence, the ultimate quality of the data. Distributed surveys have the added benefit of enabling anonymity for the participant. This provides survey participants the freedom to offer opinions without fear of reprisal or rebuttal should their opinion not conform to that of the majority or of leadership. As a rule, this means survey results are likely to be more trustworthy since they are not likely to have been influenced, though caution is warranted.

As with any measurement that relies on the opinions of human beings, the wider the pool of data, the more accurate the picture of recoverability will be. Asking only two or three individuals within a department will likely give you a very skewed or narrow perspective of the current state of preparedness. If opinions vary drastically it can become difficult to sort out which input is more valid and if the picture is really somewhere in between. Expand your audience and new patterns may emerge. Outliers will exist, but it is likely that a number of individuals will be in agreement or very close in their perceptions of some measures. As the roster grows, a consensus begins to emerge that can be counted on and serve as clear evidence of the need for improvement as well as the relative value of the program as it currently stands. Even if a clear consensus is not forthcoming, the discussion will provide everyone with very meaningful information about the organization and its level of preparedness.

Another option for obtaining these measures is via facilitated group meetings. One benefit of this approach is the relative speed by which input can be obtained. Rather than waiting weeks and sending repeated reminders following a survey request, a meeting allows the practitioner to gather input in a single session or group of sessions over the course of a day or two. In addition, consensus can be built in a group session by reducing or eliminating the disparity of responses that may exist following the survey format. You might elect to have folks answer questions prior to the meeting, and then discuss the results at the meeting, or you may elect to answer the questions for the first time together in a group. The practitioner can help the process along by answering questions about the measures and clearing up any confusion about the approach. Finally, such meetings allow the experienced practitioner to leverage his or her expertise by asking probing questions and facilitating discussion. The wise practitioner will also be able to gain important clues to the true state of affairs by reading the body language during discussion. An experienced Adaptive BC practitioner can provide a great deal of benefit in a short amount of time by properly leading discussion and getting to realistic measures.

3.3.4.1.3 Measuring Through Exercise

There is also a more involved and complex option for measuring capabilities, namely exercising. During an exercise, participants will discuss capabilities at length and the practitioner can guide the discussion to develop a robust picture of what response and recovery would look like following an actual disruption. Practitioners can use exercises to facilitate discussions about resources, procedures, and competencies or provide a forum for leadership to share existing constraints and restrictions in real time. Exercises can be developed for the primary purpose of obtaining metrics data. Consider how meaningful a series of short exercises would be that not only allowed participants the chance to explore recovery capabilities, but whose results could be used to measure the effectiveness of existing capabilities within the specific constraints of loss and restriction.

Naturally, other methods exist for BC measurement. There are even hybrid options. Surveys can be sent, then answers reviewed in a group setting to confirm or to help build consensus around the results. Data may be collected at the conclusion of an exercise when knowledge of existing resources and procedures is most clear and competency at its peak. This can then be followed up a week or two later with a survey to see if opinions have changed since and how. Participants could use a formal technique of interactive forecasting by a structured group of experts, such as the Delphi method, with individuals explaining their reasons for extreme scores as they work towards a score on which they all can agree (the method was developed originally by Rand Corporation: https://www.rand.org/topics/delphi-method.html).

There is no shortage of options for evaluating the program and obtaining measures. As with other aspects of Adaptive BC, you should feel free to be innovative in how you are able to collect data to inform your measures. At the same time, it should be clear that the primary objective is to measure the organization's ability to recover. This means that results should not be interpreted as a condemnation or unequivocal support for the program and its activities.

3.3.4.1.4 Employing the No Fault Baseline

You may wish to establish a "no fault baseline." We have found that some organizations can be punitive when anticipated results do not match actual results. It may come as quite a shock to leadership when, in shifting from counting documents to measuring capabilities, the BC program reveals significant gaps in preparedness that were never identified before! In these instances, it may be best to set the expectation that you are creating a no fault baseline. Make it clear that your BC program is trying something different, adopting a new way to measure preparedness, and as such, things may look less than desirable at first. Tell folks that you will not hold them blameworthy for existing levels of preparedness; rather, you will work with them to set and achieve new targets for improvement. This technique helps soften a potentially hard blow to the organization, especially to one that is accustomed to more traditional BC methods.

The ultimate benefit of such measures is to provide a clear snapshot of where the organization stands from a recoverability perspective. This becomes extremely useful over time as new metrics are collected and improvements demonstrated. Conversely, if changes are not having the desired effect, measurements such as these will provide a clear indicator that it is time to change direction or approach. You can also compare metrics from different departments.

Under traditional planning, such comparisons serve to shame poorly performing departments into shaping up and doing more. As we know, however, this only drives more action despite the lack of understanding as to whether such action is delivering the intended benefit. Under the Adaptive BC approach, conversely, such comparisons open the door for dialogue. The most capable departments may have more experienced leadership or simply require fewer resources. But opportunities to learn and improve abound, particularly as more data is gathered over time and across multiple parts of the organization.

3.3.4.2 Exercise Capabilities
Exercises can be used to accomplish two things at the same time: assessing and improving capabilities. As we learned in Chapter 1, we should not test for recovery time targets or to validate documented recovery scripts. This frees us to be creative and innovative in our use of exercises. The state of BC within the organization will dictate the type (e.g., tabletop, functional, or simulation), scope, and relative complexity of possible exercises. The ultimate objective of your exercise is to contribute to the improvement of each department's recoverability capabilities.

While some ideas in the following discussion might be applicable to related disciplines like emergency management, crisis management, and information technology (IT) disaster recovery, remember that we are concentrating specifically on BC and therefore specifically on BC exercises.

3.3.4.2.1 Exercise Outcomes

The practitioner should aim to achieve at least three outcomes in any exercise:

1. Increase participants' understanding of the current state of capabilities (procedures, resources, and competencies).
2. Improve participants' capabilities during the exercise itself, particularly the ability to make decisions, take action, use existing resources, and function in a post-disaster environment.
3. Identify capabilities to improve following the exercise.

3.3.4.2.2 Secondary Objectives

The practitioner may strive to achieve any one of a host of legitimate secondary objectives when running an exercise. Some may be accomplished together, while some are mutually exclusive. Examples of such secondary objectives include, but are not limited to:

- Establish or improve understanding of particular recovery capabilities that are in place.
- Give alternate personnel an opportunity to practice recovery activities in case primary designates are unavailable at time of disaster.
- Help leadership and participants to see that they are actually better prepared than they think they are.
- Help leadership and participants to see that they are not really as prepared as they think they are.
- Help leadership to see what their employees would do if senior management did not direct response activities.
- Help employees understand senior management's values, concerns, and thought processes.
- Help responders to build up their confidence to respond flexibly to disasters.
- Investigate a particular recovery strategy.
- Obtain additional data in conjunction with measuring preparedness and recoverability.
- "Stress" a particular system, service, or group of people.
- Target a particular thing, location, or group of people for loss.
- Work to build good recovery habits in individuals, reinforcing intuitive activities that contribute positively to effective recovery.

As we indicated earlier, you can take advantage of an exercise at any time during your planning work. Sometimes an exercise is a great way to engage new participants on their first day. Other times, it is a great way to conclude a full phase of planning and allow participants to see how far they have come. Exercises can be used in conjunction with measuring and baselining, or when you need to accomplish a secondary goal.

3.3.4.2.3 Applying Additional Principles Through Exercises

As you've probably guessed, exercises provide numerous opportunities to employ other Adaptive BC principles. The activity itself delivers value to those who attend. Depending on the scale and scope, you may have multiple levels of management engaged and present. This is also a good way for the practitioner to learn the business, particularly its culture and communication style. While most exercises will involve a specific scenario, this is also a time to stress that the effects or impact, not the cause, of the event should be the proper emphasis.

Exercise scenarios do not have to focus on the catastrophic either. In fact, we recommend that they do not. While there are times that it is important for participants to immerse themselves in a "smoking hole" scenario, there are other times when it is important for them to work through a more likely incident. When you are trying to build upon existing capabilities, consider exercising a common disruption such as a power outage, transit strike, or snowstorm. Work through the real business impacts, the genuine next steps, and the resources on hand to respond to the scenario. Improve upon existing capabilities and set measurable goals to close gaps.

Allow yourself to be innovative. If you have worked with your participants long enough, you should have a good sense of who they are, what they need, what they value, and what they might enjoy. You can be very creative as long as you are fulfilling your primary objective. Participants may need a very realistic scenario or something fantastic in order to create an environment in which they can relax and discover. Remind participants that now is the best time to make mistakes so they can learn and improve before a real disaster. Decisions participants make during the course of the scenario are not permanent or precedent-setting; participants should be allowed the safe space to explore potential recovery solutions. Conclude by providing closure to whatever scenario you run; you might be surprised to find that participants most often want to know how the scenario "ended." Always thank your participants for their willingness to take risks and participate.

3.3.4.3 Address Ad Hoc Opportunities

While some leaders are paragons of discipline and consistency, others are easily distracted by shiny objects and the crisis *de jour*. Regardless of the kind of leaders you work with at the departmental level, you can take advantage of opportunities to deliver value.

Ad hoc opportunities are those items loosely tied to business continuity that departmental leadership deems of value. To be blunt, this is any work you can do to build your relationship with your stakeholders while remaining true to BC principles. The more you are able to demonstrate your value by delivering quick wins, the more you will gain buy-in and respect. As Michael Watkins points out in his helpful book, *The First 90 Days*: "Early wins build your credibility and create momentum. They create virtuous cycles that leverage the energy you are putting into the organization to create a pervasive sense that good things are happening" (Watkins, 2003, p. 13).

It is important to be especially attuned to organizational culture. The individuals and cultures involved in every situation are different, and a wise practitioner will take these into account. Watkins explains: "In some companies, a win has to be a visible individual accomplishment. In others, individual pursuit of glory, even if it achieves good results, is viewed as grandstanding and destructive of teamwork.... Be sure you understand what your organization does and does not view as a win" (pp. 81-82). While it may seem almost Machiavellian, this work serves two important purposes: to maintain the support you need to get the work done, and to perform the work of continually improving recoverability capabilities.

3.3.4.3.1 Capturing Ad Hoc Opportunities
Let us look at a few examples of capturing ad hoc opportunities. These cases do not fit nicely into traditional continuity planning phases, but they further the goals of the BC program and practitioner. If you are the practitioner, make sure to take advantage of such opportunities to provide value and further your relationships with stakeholders. In many cases, these items will come up during the course of other planning activities.

- The department director is focused exclusively on communications. You can run with this focus, collecting contact information, exploring automatic notification options, testing and exercising initial notifications, setting up an intranet site for secure communication, and the like. What are the director's concerns and how can you provide value by addressing those concerns? Once you have delivered a few quick wins, and then addressed other related concerns, you can move on from communications to the next items of value.

- The director is very worried about one piece of custom-made equipment that is essential for operations and that cannot easily be replaced. This case presents a perfect opportunity for you to focus on recoverability surrounding this piece of equipment, looking at who is responsible for it, what services would be affected by its unavailability, work-around options and outsourcing possibilities. Perhaps by purchasing a second and upgraded piece of equipment, the department could double its production while also being better prepared for disaster. Perhaps you can give voice to the system failure concerns of a frontline staff member, thereby gaining further trust. By learning the business and more about this piece of equipment, you may possibly provide a good deal of primary and secondary value while making the director feel like you are really paying attention to his or her concerns.

- The director is focused on the IT systems being used. In that case, you could broker a conversation between the department and the IT folks to talk about needs, expectations, data recovery options, high availability capabilities, and likely scenarios. Clearing up misconceptions and setting proper expectations is valuable in and of itself. Moreover, this conversation may not only address some of the director's spoken and unspoken concerns, but might further empower the director with new information and connections while improving the department's recoverability capabilities.

Don't let good opportunities pass you by! In our experience, some practitioners neglect to capture and capitalize on these chances for improvement because they are focusing on a different planning activity. Consider documenting what you did and the results it had; you can demonstrate progress and value to the organization by recording improvements you completed, and you can scope out future direction by capturing improvements for later.

3.3.4.3.2 Considering Awareness

We don't talk much in this book specifically about awareness. This is primarily because we believe awareness happens as a natural byproduct of a proper planning approach. As we discussed in Chapter 1, traditional continuity planning typically tacks on awareness at the very end of its planning lifecycle, almost as an afterthought. You should be on the lookout for the many opportunities for awareness throughout your Adaptive BC work. Even an eleven-second elevator pitch can serve as a chance to develop awareness. Rather than taping up BC posters around the employee lounge every September during awareness week, look for opportunities to increase awareness as you interact with people at every level of the organization.

While this section on ad hoc opportunities is short, following these recommendations can provide a great deal of value for your BC program. Do not get so caught up in following procedure that you miss important opportunities to provide value for your stakeholders.

3.3.4.4 Improve Capabilities

This section is the trickiest of the four sets to describe, as there is the temptation to try and offer a checklist of activities. But as we stated in the introduction to this chapter, such a checklist is ill-advised in our complex and technological business world where one size does *not* fit all. Furthermore, such checklists harken back to traditional continuity methods that emphasize products over preparedness, and compliance over capability. We will try and balance the desire for specific direction with the need to adapt the approach to meet the specific requirements of your organization and its culture.

As the name implies, this section covers actions you can take to directly improve recovery capabilities. Perhaps the best help we can provide is to categorize capabilities for you. In this respect, you can encapsulate and clarify the different items to serve as the focus for improvement. Below is a categorization of recoverability capabilities with one improvement example from each subcategory:

- **Resources.**
    - o Equipment: Obtain and securely store five laptops with specialized encryption capabilities in an alternate location.

- Hardware: Obtain and install an additional firewall server to facilitate increased virtual private network (VPN) traffic.
- Software: Obtain and securely store a master copy of our customized expense tracking system.
- Staffing: Negotiate a contract for standby temporary staff with the skills necessary to staff the call center.
- Supplies: Obtain and securely store paper copies of our standard intake forms for quick retrieval at an alternate location.
- Vital records: Securely store standard operating procedures for the call center in the cloud and make them available through the Internet.
- Workspace: Convert the third floor of the call center building into an alternate office location for administrative services staff.

- **Procedures.**
  - Assess: Determine procedures for assessing and reporting the functionality of email, payroll, and human resources systems.
  - Communicate: Define who has the authority to approve communications sent directly to customers.
  - Coordinate: Assign responsibility for coordinating relocation efforts if headquarters is lost.
  - Establish locations: Document how to gain after-hours access to the call center building.
  - Mobilize: Determine where the administrative services team will meet following a disaster.
  - Prioritize: Determine who has the ultimate authority to set and reset the recovery priority of services following a disaster.

- **(Crisis) Competencies.**
  - Awareness and exercising: Hold an exercise to let the administrative services team practice their normal operations in the alternate location.
  - High performing team members: Run a Myers-Briggs assessment then bring in a consultant to interpret results and recommend next steps (see: http://www.myersbriggs.org/my-mbti-personality-type/mbti-basics/).
  - Leaders sharing vision of mission: Have leaders observe an exercise and see if their service recovery expectations match those of the responders.
  - Planning: Bring additional subject matter experts into the next planning session to obtain additional feedback and increase awareness.

In addition to working purposefully through each sub-capability to make improvements, you may also choose to work through each *loss* possibility. Begin with your set range of anticipated loss. For example, if you suddenly and unexpectedly lost certain *people*, what resources, procedures, and competencies would you need to recover each service? Within your set range of anticipated location loss, what resources, procedures, and competencies would you need to recover each service if those *locations* were lost? And what about the loss of *things*, particularly one-of-a-kind equipment and IT systems? Remember, of course, to factor in the restrictions of time, scope, and cost that you set for each service. In this way, you carefully work through the capabilities the department will need to recover at time of disaster, and always within the aperture constraints.

As you can imagine, there is an almost inexhaustible number of improvements that can be made with regard to recoverability. How to identify them, how deeply to investigate, and how many to implement are naturally dependent upon you, the department, and the organization. The value of an experienced Adaptive BC practitioner is that he or she will be able to balance the needs of the BC program with the needs of the organization to find the right approach for each department. No Internet template can provide this proper guidance.

3.3.4.5 Improve your Customized Response Portfolios
A quote from Sun Tzu's *Art of War* feels cliché in a business book, but this particular quote caught our attention nonetheless: "Now the general who wins a battle makes many calculations in his temple ere the battle is fought. The general who loses a battle makes but few calculations beforehand. Thus do many calculations lead to victory, and few calculations to defeat: how much more no calculation at all!" (Sun Tzu, 1.26).

When you are planning, ask yourself, "How important is it to recover this service following disaster?" While the answer to that question will depend on a host of factors, the more important it is to recover a service, the more you and your participants will have to brainstorm, imagine, and strategize. Sports, military, law enforcement, airlines, and many other types of organizations take this topic very seriously. In these industries, you can bet people spend a great deal of time thinking through what-if scenarios and calculating their various outcomes.

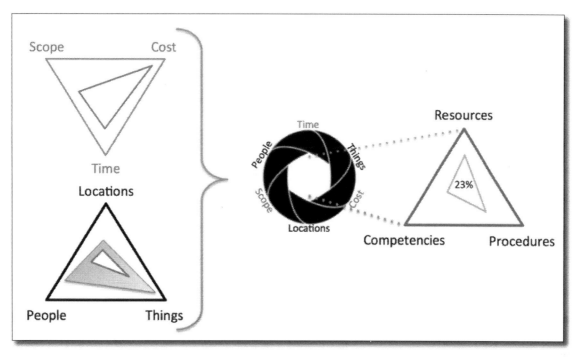

Figure 3-2. Capability and Constraint Model

What are the specific loss impacts a disaster could have on this department? How would we utilize our capabilities to overcome each of these impacts? These two questions can serve as the beginning of an effort to consider particular loss outcomes and develop a portfolio of responses customized to the needs of a particular department. Naturally, you can use the capability and constraint model in Figure 3-2 that was explained in Chapter 2 as your guide, identifying the specific losses that might happen in each category and thinking through how the department would handle that situation. For example:

- **Loss of things:** If the payroll system was unavailable, we could have the bank rerun last month's payroll (procedure) because they have both the data and the equipment (resources) and it would be easy for them (competencies); we would then have to reconcile (procedure) when the payroll system came back online.

- **Loss of people:** If Mike and Sally landed in the hospital because they went out to lunch and ate bad potato salad, we could reach out to Fred over in accounting (procedure) who used to work here (competencies) with our systems (resources) and we could have him do just the bare essentials (procedure) until Mike and Sally got back.

- **Loss of locations:** If the third floor flooded out because a pipe burst, then we might lose access to room 205; we could relocate the six employees (procedure) across the street to the call center (resources) and they would have the phones and workstations (resources) they need to just work as normal (competencies) as everything they need is in the cloud (resources).

After working with a department for a while, you will learn its weak spots and its strengths. Explore the weaknesses and what would happen if they were affected. Think about ways to leverage the department's strengths during a disaster as well. As the book *StrengthsFinder 2.0* points out, it can be more advantageous to improve upon things you do well than to try to improve things you do not (Rath, 2007). Perhaps you can find ways to use strengths to overcome weakness in recovery.

Apply the principles from the manifesto:

- Document only for mnemonics – create cheat sheets and reference guides, not binders of instructions.
- Develop your business acumen and bring it to bear when coming up with what-if scenarios and their potential impacts.
- As we are no longer encumbered by a detailed business impact analysis, be creative in coming up with workarounds and solutions to add to your recovery portfolio.
- Get people from different parts of the department (and outside of the department) to participate in brainstorming and exercising.

When recovery is essential, you want to develop a thorough portfolio of possible responses customized just for the specific needs of individual departments. As Howard Mannella stated simply during a personal interview in 2014, your job is to create a "portfolio of activities that can be activated selectively and scaled accordingly." These responses will fall within the aperture of loss and restrictions, and will be made up of capabilities. Department leaders will work to increase the number of possible responses along with the resources and competencies that support these responses. The more important it is to recover the service, the more what-if loss scenarios you will want to consider and the more robust a response portfolio you will want to put in place. Then, when disaster strikes, department leaders will use the most appropriate responses from the portfolio, mixing and matching as needed, to meet the demands of the situation. You are working to be adaptive, not only in your planning efforts, but in your response efforts as well!

As the ancient Chinese military writer Sun Tzu noted, in a modern translation, "If generals do not know how to adapt advantageously, even if they know the lay of the land they cannot take advantage of it" (Sun Tzu, 1988, p.128).

3.3.5 Refine

As the practitioner establishes constraints ("sets the aperture") and improves capabilities, a natural interplay develops between these activities. Changes and discoveries while improving capabilities will influence decisions about constraints. Changing the levels of constraints will influence capabilities. Thus, the practitioner continues to refine settings to the aperture and measurements of capabilities, shifting focus between capabilities and constraints and adjusting both as planning moves forward. This may be particularly so while the practitioner moves between areas and departments within the organization, gaining insight into the business of the business, and applying information learned from one service to work with another. One department's constraints may affect another's assumptions; strategies to improve one service's capabilities may affect another's constraints. The model's inherent flexibility allows for continual modification of constraints and prioritization of investments in capabilities. Such adjustments are not just based on new data and dependencies, but also on changes within the organization, such as operational priorities, available capital, sensitivity to markets, and new regulations.

There is an analogy here with modern (digital) photography. The professional photographer sets the aperture of her camera and takes a picture. She then examines the picture and edits it with computer software. Based on these edits, she learns the best settings for her camera, changes the aperture, and re-takes the picture. This process continues until she is satisfied that the result meets the requirements of her customer, and then she prints the image. As she moves on to other assignments, she continues to learn the best aperture settings and best editing strategies to create the best images. There is a continual, if not always visible, interplay between aperture settings and the imaging strategies. So too does the professional planner make adjustments based on the interplay between constraints and capabilities.

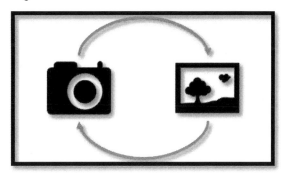

Figure 3-3. Refining a Photograph

Refinement is not a single step that you perform at any one time. Refinement, like many other Adaptive BC principles and activities, runs through all your initiatives. The best professionals will always be on the lookout for ways to improve their planning efforts. Perhaps a source of post-disaster funding for one department can be used in another. Perhaps a restriction uncovered in one area should be applied across the organization. Refinement also speaks to the nonlinear and parallel nature of the Adaptive BC approach, which we specifically address next.

3.4 The Nonlinear and Parallel Nature of Adaptive BC

At this point, if you are asking yourself, "What is the right order in which to perform these activities?" then perhaps you have not been paying enough attention.

The culture, needs, mission, situation, market, personalities, interests, and a host of other factors will inform the thoughtful Adaptive BC practitioner on how to structure his or her approach for each step for each department. You cannot identify a proper order for these activities without knowing and learning about the organization in an iterative and continuous improvement cycle.

Furthermore, these activities are both nonlinear and parallel. By *nonlinear* we mean that no one activity is dependent on any other activity and that there is no necessary sequence. You can perform any activity in any order without jeopardizing the planning effort. We also mean that initial results will inform your work to create future results, like a feedback loop. Past results will factor into future steps. By *parallel*, we mean that planning and preparedness activities can be performed at practically the same time. You will discover ad hoc opportunities during many different activities. You should frequently discuss iterations and next steps. Any meeting can be an opportunity to raise awareness, and so forth. Remember that all the principles of the manifesto apply so any one activity is an opportunity to holistically encompass many objectives.

3.4.1 Dealing with Order of Execution

In this chapter, we presented Adaptive BC activities in the following order:

- **Set direction.**
  - o Set program direction.
  - o Set departmental level direction (including loss constraints).
  - o Identify services (including restrictions).
  - o Kickoff/regroup.
  - o Set iterations.
- **Improve capabilities.**
  - o Assess capabilities.
  - o Exercise capabilities.
  - o Address ad hoc opportunities.
  - o Improve capabilities (and address loss constraints).
  - o Improve your customized response portfolios.
- **Refine.**

But this order is not prescriptive. For example, taking all factors into account, your first six months of work with a single department might look like this:

Exercise → Assess → Set departmental direction → Directly improve capabilities → Kickoff → Directly improve capabilities → Set iterations → Identify services → Improve your response portfolio → Set iterations → Directly improve capabilities → Assess → Exercise → Set departmental direction (and you are always refining!)

It begins to look complex, and properly so. The Adaptive BC approach must be simple enough to get started, but robust enough to handle the most sophisticated of operations. At the end of the day, there are really only two things you must remember – your job is to:

- Set and refine the aperture.
- Assess and improve capabilities (within the aperture).

How you do this is ultimately up to you.

3.4.2 Can I Do This My Own Way?

James Goebel, an early practitioner and thought leader of what became Agile project management, gave a bit of practical wisdom during a presentation in the 1990s. To paraphrase:

- If it is working, do more of it.
- If it is not working, do less of it.
- If you don't know whether it's working or not, do little experiments.

In this chapter, we have tried to provide you with a systematic approach that has worked for us and other practitioners at many different organizations across the globe. While we are a bit skeptical about "best practices," we are very fond of *proven* practices. As we argued in Chapter 1, we believe that traditional BC practices simply do not work. They are focused on doing the wrong things in the wrong way and do not provide enough value. We think the approach presented in this chapter, the capability and constraint model of recoverability shown in Figure 3-2 and explained in Chapter 2, the examples in Chapter 4, and the recommendations in Chapter 5, together provide an effective and efficient alternative to traditional continuity planning.

Unlike the practices of the discipline's past that have gone virtually unchanged for decades, we anticipate change in Adaptive BC. Times will change. Technology, business practices, market composition, and worldview will change. You will have to experiment with this approach to find what works best for you and the services you support. Naturally we recommend starting with the approach we have outlined above, but you should feel free to change the terms, steps, scope, and practice of the above outcomes. And, if you are so inclined, reach out to others in the profession (and us!) to share what you've learned. Ultimately, the more sophisticated in the theory and practice of business continuity we all become, the better we will be at safeguarding our friends, families, and communities. In the meantime, let us move on to Chapter 4 where we provide suggestions and examples for bringing all this together in your daily practice.

References

The annotated art of war (Part 1.26: Calculations). (n.d.). Retrieved from
   http://changingminds.org/disciplines/warfare/art_war/sun_tzu_1-6.htm

Rath, T. (2007). *StrengthsFinder 2.0*. New York, NY: Gallup Press.

Sun Tzu. (1988). *The art of war* (T. Cleary, Trans.). Boston, MA: Shambhala.

Watkins, M. (2003). *The first 90 days: Critical success strategies for new leaders at all
   levels*. Boston, MA: Harvard Business School.

Chapter 4

Finishing

Chapter 3 dug into the practical execution of Adaptive Business Continuity (Adaptive BC). This chapter also looks at practical execution, but by way of narrative examples. Here we will demonstrate Adaptive BC "in action." We will introduce you to five fictional practitioners who manage business continuity (BC) at five different organizations. Each practitioner works in a different industry, with varying corporate cultures, reporting up to a different part of the organization. Each example presents a practitioner faced with a different set of challenges and then details how such challenges can be tackled using an Adaptive BC approach. In this way, we hope that you will get a better idea of how to implement the Adaptive BC principles in your own program.

While these organizations and practitioners are completely fictitious, the methods used to tackle the various challenges of each are based on the real-world experiences of practitioners in actual organizations. Long before this book was written, there were professionals in the industry who recognized the need to do things differently. We have taken and synthesized these stories involving unique challenges in order to demonstrate how the Adaptive BC approach could be used to improve and benefit any BC program.

This chapter will help you to:

- Understand how Adaptive BC can be effective in organizations with vastly different cultures and program maturity levels.
- Learn how to apply Adaptive BC approaches in a variety of different settings.
- Think through some typical challenges and opportunities that may arise while implementing an Adaptive BC approach.
- See, through case studies, how you might execute the Adaptive BC framework in different ways to meet challenges at different organizations.

4.1 Examples and Approaches

The purpose of the case studies in this chapter is to demonstrate some of the genuine challenges that BC practitioners deal with on a regular basis, and how they use Adaptive BC solutions to meet those challenges. We have given each hypothetical organization multiple issues for the professional to contend with. We then outline a specific approach the fictional BC practitioner employs at that organization and conclude with outcomes and lessons learned. Our example solutions do not necessarily represent the absolute best of all possible methods, but we present them this way to highlight the advantages of the Adaptive BC approach in tackling a variety of situations.

In all cases, we can assume our practitioners are experienced professionals in the BC discipline. All of them, like nearly all of us, took the traditional path of learning and applying traditional BC practices. In all cases, our practitioners struggled to deliver value quickly and effectively using the widely accepted methods of execution. Through research and discussions with peers, they came across the Adaptive BC Manifesto, related articles, and materials. Eventually they interacted with other like-minded practitioners at conferences, on phone calls, and through discussion groups. Like many real-life practitioners, they were pleased to discover that others in their profession had the same struggles and that alternative approaches existed.

Each practitioner follows an approach within Adaptive BC that is suited to his or her strengths and skillsets. Each has independently learned about the capabilities and constraints model of recoverability; the resources, procedures, and competencies model of measurement; and setting the aperture. In addition, different practices are implemented based on the individual organization each serves. For instance, in regulated environments or where leadership is already familiar with traditional planning concepts, some re-education has to take place. In other institutions, Adaptive BC can be implemented without having to change mindsets or convince executives of the value of doing things the Adaptive BC way.

Adaptive BC is meant to be extremely flexible. With time and experience we expect capable BC professionals to be able to modify the framework to fit their own unique environment. We hope that as you read through these examples you will recognize your own employer or culture while envisioning solutions within Adaptive BC that will benefit your own program. While we present five different examples with five different labels for each approach, they are not meant to be comprehensive or exclusive. They are:

1. A neo-traditional scenario at Widgets, Inc.
2. A neo-compliance scenario at Big Money Bank.
3. A service-centric scenario at GlitzCorp.
4. A capabilities-focused scenario at PeopleMovers, Inc.
5. An exercise-first scenario at Stuff2Buy.

4.2 Case Study #1: Taking a Neo-Traditional Approach
4.2.1 Widgets, Inc.
Widgets, Inc. is a family owned and operated manufacturing company with a 100-plus year history. Widgets, Inc. has grown in recent years through acquisitions resulting in many disparate parts of the organization that tend to operate independently. From a BC perspective, nothing formal has been developed or put into place. There has been little exposure to BC practices or terminology. But a recent technology mishap has opened management's eyes to the need for improved recoverability. While the leaders at Widgets, Inc. are supportive, many of them are slow to change. They are eager to learn but sometimes get distracted by high-profile events around them and their perspective is informed only by their direct experience with the recent technology outage.

4.2.2 Meet George: Widgets, Inc.'s Business Continuity Manager
George was recently hired by Widgets, Inc. to fill a new role: business continuity manager. The role was created within corporate safety and security following the technology outage. George is a people-oriented individual who is less focused on policy, process, and procedures. He prefers to work face-to-face in order to build positive relationships and develop competency rather than creating materials. George will be tasked with building an enterprise BC program from scratch.

George has a lot of experience leading BC programs following widely accepted practices and has experimented with Adaptive BC practices in the past, but this is his first attempt at building a program from scratch following the Adaptive BC framework. Knowing that executives at Widgets, Inc. have no familiarity with traditional practices means George can follow this path without expectations that deliverables, such as the business impact analysis (BIA) and risk assessment (RA), will be produced. As far as leadership at Widgets, Inc. is concerned, this is how BC is conducted.

George has chosen a path that we will call "neo-traditional," because, on the surface, it looks a bit like a BC approach that follows the traditional BC lifecycle. Of the five examples in this chapter, we begin with this one because it most closely resembles the priorities of traditional BC planning and will likely feel the most comfortable to experienced practitioners. Let's take a look at George's adoption of the Adaptive BC approach and see how he does.

4.2.3 Starting with Incident Response
At the outset, George sees an opportunity to rapidly improve the organization's overall recoverability with the implementation of a proper incident response process. Since senior leaders just suffered through an event for which they were poorly prepared, this presents an opportunity to provide demonstrable value in an area that is also a topic of interest. Done correctly, George will help build credibility and support for his future endeavors.

During the interview process, George learns a lot from his manager Terry, the VP for corporate safety and security. George is told that the company experienced a serious disruption just three months prior. The outage was the result of a power failure within their data center environment. Because all the server equipment suffered a "hard" crash, one critical piece of hardware could not be adequately recovered. Systems were eventually brought online but it was a slow and painful process. It took nearly three days to restore all system connections and dependencies. Senior management was alarmed not just by how poorly prepared they were from a technology perspective but how entirely reliant they were upon systems to run their operations. They also worry that their lack of familiarity with technology means capabilities and threats can be easily, and even deliberately, obfuscated. This is leadership's reasoning for putting business continuity within safety and security, instead of technology, where a BC manager might become too technology-focused. George takes it as a very positive sign that senior leadership is open to focusing on BC issues in parallel with information technology (IT) disaster recovery gaps.

The first week is extremely fast-paced. Terry personally introduces George to many department managers, spending several afternoons walking with George from office to office. During introductions, George tries to glean some general information without imposing too much. He spends almost all of his time listening and not talking. He takes note of existing capabilities to build upon later. George ends the week asking Terry what senior management's expectations are and how he should report the progress he makes. He inquires about tools and systems that may be in place to facilitate communications, meetings, and collaboration.

Over the course of the second week on the job, George contacts each of the operational presidents to introduce himself and learn a little more about the products and services performed in each manufacturing location. There are six different plants across the country, plus the corporate offices. As part of some of the brief conversations, George learns some valuable information that will help when he tackles service recovery later on. For the short-term, though, George will keep his main focus on establishing a proper incident and event response process.

George's initial discussions have helped him set a preliminary aperture for planning purposes. Because George is starting with incident response, the aperture is not a primary consideration. He knows that any disruptive incident will result in execution of the event response process, often before the scope of impact can be adequately determined. This means that even those events that are outside of the defined scope of the aperture will still need to follow the process in order for leaders to make decisions about execution of response strategies. This process also sets the stage for participants to understand their roles and familiarize themselves with the wide range of disruptive events, many of them small or relatively minor, to which they may be needed to respond.

George forms local incident response teams at each of the remote manufacturing facilities. He solicits members at each site to take responsibility for safety, security, facilities, communications, and technology. He also assigns an incident commander role that is filled by the local VP of operations. As part of the initiative he writes up an overview of responsibilities for each role and a high-level process for how the team will be alerted to potential issues, how they will assemble if conditions warrant, and what they will do upon activation. The vast majority of team members are willing to fulfill the roles defined for them.

4.2.4 A Brief Detour

During this second week, the chief human resources officer at Widgets Inc., Dr. Fields, contacts George. She has been hearing a lot about a pandemic threat in the south of the country. Neither George nor Terry consider this an immediate threat to the organization. George would prefer to work quickly to implement a broader program without focusing on specific threats. But after speaking with Dr. Fields, George recognizes an opportunity to build a relationship while improving the organization's recovery capabilities. He makes time to perform these few quick activities:

- First, working with his counterparts in safety and security, he contacts some external suppliers about protective supplies like hand sanitizers, gloves, and masks as well as materials that can be used to promote good practices like washing hands and sneezing properly to avoid spreading germs.
- Second, he works with the human resources (HR) department to craft emergency policies that can be implemented in response to an event. This includes specific rules to enable social distancing like virtual meetings, guidance for employees working from home, and how to handle personal time off.
- Last, he uses this opportunity to better define HR's role in the incident response process while expanding and generalizing the defined pandemic response to include all nature of threats and impacts.

While this work shifts his focus away from incident response for a while, he builds a good relationship with several members of the HR team, learns more about HR's role in a disaster, and identifies additional resources he could bring to bear during an event. Perhaps most importantly, he has gained an ally in the chief HR officer by quickly producing value for an initiative she felt was important.

Following the work above, George returns to his incident response focus. Working with the other team members he builds support for a defined process to respond rapidly to a variety of issues. This means that the safety, security, and facilities team members who are already practiced in working collaboratively can help lead and educate their fellow team members. George also facilities a few brief exercises with each of the teams to discuss their responses to different types of events. George suspects there are some weaknesses in the ability of desktop support, transportation, and logistics to respond effectively in a post-disaster situation, so he creates scenarios to stress these particular areas. As part of this work, George builds upon existing safety response capabilities to include instructions for alerting managers to threats and disruptions.

4.2.5 Service Recovery

While his first order of business was addressing incident response, George believes the next step that will provide the most value will be improving service-level recovery at the six manufacturing plants. The vast majority of Widgets, Inc.'s workforce and resources are dedicated to manufacturing specific products for delivery to distributors across the country. The six different plants produce several dozen products in hundreds of variations.

Terry and George decide to start with a tight scope of work for this phase, focusing specifically on the potential loss of one of Widgets, Inc.'s buildings due to a localized incident. Because the complete loss of a manufacturing plant is both a possibility as well as something from which the organization can be expected to recover, this marks the upper end of the aperture for recovery from the loss of locations, as opposed to loss of all six plants. Some of the information George needs was gleaned from initial discussions during incident response improvements. George needs only three weeks to follow up with individual managers in order to obtain the additional details he needs to move forward. George also makes these important discoveries:

- A majority of products can be produced at multiple locations.
- Widgets, Inc. generally maintains a solid 30-day lead time; so even absent the ability to manufacture, it will be 30 days or more before customers are impacted in the event of a loss of manufacturing capability.
- Two particularly critical items produced by Widgets, Inc. can only be made at one specific location.
- Widgets, Inc. contracts with distributors for delivery of products directly to consumers; such contracts generally include service level agreements that specify lead times and product quality.

This informs the next phase of the effort: improvement. Improvement opportunities are split into three categories: resources, procedures, and competencies. The work is then prioritized based on those improvements that have the greatest impact for the least effort or lowest investment. Over the next four weeks, George oversees the development of procedures for the execution of some strategies based on capabilities that already exist for each area. At the same time, he works with leaders at each of the manufacturing locations to identify individuals with the knowledge and experience to fill key roles in the event of a disruption. Naturally, no single plan works for all six locations; George has to be responsive to the differences between the people, cultures, and missions at each location, partnering with folks to craft a plan that will actually be used by the responders.

4.2.6 Tackling Challenges

One of George's most daunting challenges is working with the vastly different personality types and priorities of Widgets, Inc.'s various operational leaders. One such leader – Michael – was a long-standing vice president at his company prior to it being bought by Widgets, Inc. Michael is proud of his part of the organization and feels it is the best run, maintains the highest quality, and experiences the fewest issues and outages. In his mind, avoiding issues means not having outages to respond to. Some of Michael's staff feel very differently from Michael, particularly the plant manager, and George works with many of them directly. The plant manager happens to be Michael's most trusted employee and George works through her to get most of the approvals needed from Michael and gain support from the rest of the team.

One of the most important results of George's work overall is that managers now have an understanding of the organization's recovery capabilities and where a few basic steps can greatly improve on those capabilities. In one area, George worked with vice presidents to obtain additional resources. In another area, he partnered with Dr. Fields to run some team-building exercises and leadership style evaluations to develop crisis competencies. In a third area, the planning group worked through high-level recovery steps for the replacement of a particular piece of plastic injection molding equipment that they felt was key to their operation. In each instance, George worked in rapid iterations to provide deliverables that not only furthered the BC program but also provided specific value to particular groups in the organization.

4.2.7 Outcome

Let us take a step back and summarize George's successes up to this point. In the first four months, George accomplished the following:

- He greatly improved incident response and took the first steps towards closing significant gaps in service-level recovery.
- He identified services for recovery and even started to target improvement opportunities in the event of a loss of a manufacturing location.
- He established a positive relationship with the HR department by partnering with the executive leader and involving the team in helping to improve crisis competencies.
- He established a reputation for partnership and action.

At the end of this first four months, George met with executive leaders to inform them of the progress made and to outline next steps. He did not meet to obtain their buy-in and approval, though he did make a request for the purchase of plant equipment to enable the production of some specific products at other locations. In this case, the equipment was fairly inexpensive and was used to replace aging items at the proposed plant. By learning the business of the business, George was informed of a particularly popular product manufactured at only one location. Improving the ability to recover the manufacture of this product by also producing it at another location will improve distribution times and increase sales.

There is still work to be done and George makes a point of bringing up two key items that have yet to be addressed:

1. The technology environment is still at risk and George will have to try to get resources to own and manage IT disaster recovery.
2. The support departments, such as finance and HR, have not taken any steps to improve and that will be George's next step to review and improve.

Armed with several quick wins and the funding needed to complete additional initiatives, George now feels confident that his accomplishments will lay the foundation for the next round of measurable improvements to the organization's recovery capabilities. Executive leadership is now interested in the deliverables from George's proposed next step, namely an enterprise-wide, baseline measurement of existing recovery capabilities.

4.2.8 Lessons Learned

Let's look at what George and others at Widgets, Inc. learned through the use of Adaptive BC principles and approaches:

- By focusing on incident management at the outset, this particular organization is much better prepared to deal effectively with any disruptive event that comes along. This work was completed relatively quickly by eliminating a lot of up-front analysis that provides little value in getting such capabilities off the ground.
- George's initial focus on the process left individual and team competencies unaddressed and at some risk. By engaging the HR teams to develop crisis competencies, this should be less of an issue moving forward.
- By addressing the concern of Dr. Fields, George developed additional credibility at the executive level.
- By postponing executive engagement until he had some accomplishments to deliver, George established a reputation for action. At the same time, his meeting with leadership was not around support and buy-in for the program but to obtain approval and take action towards improving the organization's overall recoverability, further cementing George's dedication to action and avoiding time-wasting activities.
- Support areas are still at significant risk – the interrelated nature of these internal services means they could impact recovery following a significant disruption. George's positive relationship with HR leadership will help in tackling that function and may enable further engagement of other support function leaders.
- The initial driver to bring George onboard was the recent technology outage. This part of the organization still has not taken any demonstrable action. Hopefully, George's work can expand to cover this critical part of Widgets, Inc. and he will be successful in getting resources dedicated to this effort.

4.2.9 Case Study #1: Conclusion

We named this the neo-traditional scenario, since it shares high-level similarities with traditional BC lifecycle approaches, starting with incident response planning and moving on to service recovery strategies. But note the differences – George did not do the following:

- Conduct a risk assessment or a business impact analysis. Instead, in a fraction of the time that it would have taken to perform these steps, George made significant improvements in recovery.
- Define recovery time or recovery point objectives. At no time did the teams involved work towards specific time targets.
- Wait to obtain senior-level approval before diving in and delivering value. He partnered with many people from different parts of the organization, turning quick wins into business value and relationship capital.
- Try to create "the plan" for recovery. He documented only to help people remember the decisions they had made and the potential information they might wish to reference following a disaster. Procedures were only one of three elements that George focused on, spending time to shore up resources and improve crisis competencies as well.
- Try to push a one-size-fits-all approach onto everyone at every location. George met people where they were in their culture, history, and preparedness, starting with existing capabilities and working to improve.

Not too bad for fourteen weeks of work!

4.3 Case Study #2: Taking a Neo-Compliance Approach
4.3.1 Big Money Bank

Big Money Bank is a regional financial institution that primarily operates in the consumer banking and lending space. This includes consumer and small business banking as well as mortgage, auto, and non-secured consumer lending. This institution was primarily a regional player but recently acquired two other companies to expand its reach to other markets. The originating company operated almost as a small business but recent expansion and acquisition opportunities have meant some changes in leadership and introduced different cultures into the organization. Because this is a regulated industry, leadership has some familiarity with traditional BC practices.

4.3.2 Meet Elizabeth: Big Money Bank's Director of Enterprise BC

Elizabeth was hired as the director of enterprise BC. This role reports to the director of information security, and Elizabeth replaces Chuck who left around the time of the acquisitions. Elizabeth is a go-getter who is not afraid to approach senior leadership with new ideas and input. With several different leaders from multiple, recently merged organizations, her style suits the situation at hand.

Elizabeth has followed traditional BC practices in the past and is familiar with the deliverables expected from regulators. Elizabeth was successful running a program following Adaptive BC principles at her previous employer. In that role there were no regulatory requirements to meet, so she is naturally concerned with how Adaptive BC will be received by external auditors of the program. She has seen, first-hand, the value of the Adaptive BC framework and feels confident that she can demonstrate that it makes for overall better preparedness, engagement, and recoverability. But she also knows that many auditors and regulators have little familiarity with BC outside of the requirements dictated to them by recognized standards. As a result, some auditors can be rigid in their interpretation and provide little leeway in executing continuity activities.

Elizabeth is further challenged with taking a very traditional BC program and modifying it for the times ahead while also expanding it to include the new parts of the organization. We've titled the scenario here "neo-compliance" because Elizabeth's main challenge is to satisfy regulatory requirements while also dealing with the acquisition and working to continuously improve the bank's overall recovery capabilities. Let's see how she uses an Adaptive BC approach to meet her objectives and provide value to the company.

4.3.3 Obtaining Incremental Direction from Leadership

With the recent acquisition and varying cultures, Elizabeth believes it is best to speak with leadership first. Given that Elizabeth plans to change the approach to BC from how Chuck used to do it, she feels it is a good idea to bring executive management into the process early. While this is not a requirement of the Adaptive BC approach, both the culture of Big Money Bank and the anticipated regulatory expectations make leadership awareness important in this case.

Rather than forming a steering committee, or waiting for a time where she can make a big pitch to all the executives, Elizabeth meets with each leader separately. She keeps these conversations informal in order to build rapport and set the stage for future meetings. Elizabeth spends the majority of the time in these brief meetings focused on learning what, specifically, is known and expected of her BC program, particularly in the new, combined organization.

What Elizabeth learns is of little surprise. In past years the BC program at Big Money Bank followed a traditional approach. This meant an emphasis on heavy documentation and formal, committee-driven meetings that included review and approval of materials for the purpose of satisfying regulatory requirements. The anticipated increase in regulatory scrutiny because of the acquisitions is also having a negative effect on the leadership team. This has manifested itself in increased secrecy and safeguarding of program issues and deficiencies. It also means the executive team's intention is not only to continue following standard practices but also to increase the emphasis on documentation in order to avoid regulatory findings. In one discussion, Elizabeth is instructed to focus, almost exclusively, on satisfying regulators.

The recently acquired companies, by contrast, are smaller and less heavily regulated. This means Elizabeth spends more time informing the leaders about BC than she intended. On the positive side, this is an opportunity to shape their expectations of her program and the value it can provide. She emphasizes the need to deliver value as well as put capabilities above documentation.

Elizabeth decides that her biggest challenge will be addressing the legacy portion of Big Money Bank that prefers to follow a regulatory-driven, check-the-box approach to BC. Convincing management to follow a new approach at a time of significant change poses a serious test of her abilities. She plans on preemptively building credibility through introductions by executive leadership to quickly get time on mid-management's calendars and start talking. This will enable her to build support at several different levels of the organization, working "bottom-up" and "top-down" simultaneously.

4.3.4 Engaging at All Levels and Establishing Baselines

Recognizing that BIAs and RAs provide little value to executives, participants, or her objectives, yet acknowledging that they are a regulatory requirement, Elizabeth sets out to satisfy these requirements in the least amount of time. Every minute a bank member spends filling out a BIA spreadsheet is a minute that could be better used to improve recovery capabilities. She creates new BIA and RA templates that are significantly reduced in scope. She concentrates on getting participants to identify and categorize their department's services in a meaningful way. She does not waste time trying to quantify impacts or time targets; though, to satisfy anticipated compliance requirements, she does have participants highlight their most critical services. The results provide Elizabeth with insight into how different departments view their mission, their products, and the relative criticality of their services. In the end, she spends a fraction of the normal time and produces lightweight documents that she hopes will satisfy auditors.

At this point, Elizabeth has one primary objective: establish a baseline measurement of recoverability. A quantitative baseline provides both an objective metric of the organization's preparedness while also aiding in the determination of priorities for future efforts. In the interest of time, Elizabeth performs group meetings with all the managers in each department. Elizabeth uses the discussions to achieve many secondary objectives. First, discussions are a means to learn the business further. Discussions can also help to build a common understanding and arrive at some baseline measures. To do this, Elizabeth questions what management has in place and what each would do in the event of a loss of the primary facility. She explores whether the employees have experience with real disasters and if they have practiced any recovery procedures. The discussions that take place fulfill the final objective: to build collaborative teams, thereby improving the department's competencies, even if just a little.

Ahead of each meeting, Elizabeth briefly surveys participants about their perception of the department's competencies: Does everyone have a good understanding of resources and procedures available to them? Do team members communicate and collaborate effectively? Do they have skills and experience to effectively respond and recover in the event of a major disaster?

At the conclusion of each meeting, Elizabeth passes the same survey around again. The results from the second survey often indicate that the groups are beginning to recognize their deficiencies and the gaps that need to be overcome in the months ahead. In some cases, the second surveys shows an improvement over the results of the first; this serves as evidence that even something as basic as a group meeting can benefit the organization's recovery capability.

In many cases, teams also identify steps that can be taken to quickly close obvious or easy gaps. In one example, Stephanie, the call center manager, complains that her team members rarely take their devices home because they do not have laptop bags. Such bags do not seem like an essential resource to the others in the meeting, but Stephanie explains that employees do not just need a laptop but also a power cord, a headset, and multiple other items. Taking all these home means hand-carrying a lot of small items that can easily be lost, misplaced, or broken. Elizabeth addresses this by contacting the marketing department and obtaining a relatively inexpensive quote for a set of 40 laptop bags that Stephanie immediately approves. In another example, the technology team discovers that their offshore support partners rely on a single piece of hardware within the data center. While their critical applications are redundant, offshore staff will be unable to access them through their virtual desktops if the data center were ever to become unavailable. Upon this discovery, Keith, the technical service desk manager, takes it upon himself to close the gap, something that Elizabeth follows up on two months later.

At the conclusion of this effort, Elizabeth returns to leadership, having brief follow-up conversations with the senior managers she had met with several weeks prior. Where initial conversations were used to obtain information, this next round provides Elizabeth the opportunity to share details around the company's state of preparedness, communicate the improvements that have taken place, and determine the priorities for further preparedness efforts. She provides leadership with the first baseline of its kind in the company. While some executives remain as relatively disinterested as before, others are quickly warming up to her approach.

4.3.5 Maximizing Quick Wins and Delivering Continuous Value
Elizabeth uses a combination of measurement and extremely quick wins to build a foundation before going on to more significant improvement activities. Now that she is working to directly improve recovery capabilities, she makes sure to set the planning aperture. Elizabeth identified some specific constraints, including:

- Very short time commitments for wire transmissions.
- Relaxed rules for response to regulatory issues in the event of a crisis.
- The lack of capital available for post-disaster response following the recent acquisitions.

Based on her follow-up executive meetings, Elizabeth is able to validate her next improvement priorities. Among the improvements that need to be addressed quickly are:
- The recovery capability of wire services within the combined organization.
- The ability to recover critical technology resources.
- The overall response capability within the three institutions during the acquisition period where recovery may be complicated due to the ongoing changes.

The redundancy of operations between the three organizations makes the recoverability of wire transfers an easy target for improvement. In one instance, Elizabeth helps Big Money Bank develop modified rules for the Federal Reserve to accept transfers on behalf of Big Money Bank by one of its partners under acquisition. Employees at the partner institution practice procedures so that they can effectively carry out transfers for Big Money Bank, if necessary. In another instance, the finance department develops a long-term project to consolidate all processing but maintain redundancy of operations. Elizabeth works with the managers in finance to establish a regular cadence of exercising to ensure staff remain familiar with the process.

The primary challenge Elizabeth faces for her second goal is ensuring that critical systems in the consolidated environment maintain the same level of recoverability or better both during and after the acquisition activities. In most cases, Big Money Bank plans to maintain the systems it uses while sunsetting redundant applications used at the acquired companies. This means ensuring that any improvements to performance or additions to capacity applied to production systems are carried over to the recovery environment. In a few instances, Big Money Banks's applications will be turned down in favor of lower cost or better performing systems used by the smaller institutions being taken over. Elizabeth seeks out and establishes a relationship with the project management team leadership and even manages to make herself part of the committee overseeing acquisition-related changes. Through this, she obtains access to all project management-related systems and is added to the weekly change distribution list.

Improving initial response capabilities proves to be the most daunting of the three goals because response procedures are so disparate among the three institutions. To further complicate matters, none of the organizations have ever executed or even practiced an initial response. Elizabeth tackles this particular shortcoming by meeting with managers over the primary areas that might receive awareness of an emergency or disaster: technical support, safety and security, and facilities. Each organization, it turns out, has different processes, procedures, and intakes for these. One company, for example, outsources its alarm monitoring and reporting. This includes a third-party security command center. In another instance, no centralized group exists: Technical support is primarily handled by the desktop support team though the application and engineering teams are also on-call and routinely field calls of all sorts, including reports of emergencies.

In trying to figure out a way to quickly improve this messy situation, Elizabeth learns that Big Money Banks's technical operations team works 24x7, providing "level one" support and escalating to the appropriate groups as necessary. Elizabeth takes two significant steps to consolidate response under a single umbrella. First, she works with the project management team to accelerate the support of the newly acquired companies by Big Money Bank's technical operations group. Second, she works with the operations director to expand the responsibilities of that group to include escalation and reporting of safety, security, and facilities related issues. She experiences significant pushback at first but, through group meetings involving the corporate life safety, security, and facilities leaders and the operations director, finally satisfies any major concerns over the increased scope of ownership. All support teams report that their level of critical engagements and communications is limited (at most, four or five a week). This result satisfies the operations director that the level of work for that group will not increase significantly, and scripts are developed to quickly notify and escalate such situations to the appropriate parties.

The final step in the process is some functional testing which consists of Elizabeth and others placing calls to numerous individuals and teams in order to see if they follow the process as defined. In a few weeks, participants have identified existing resources, created meaningful procedures, and enhanced crisis competencies in the organization to the point where everyone feels demonstrably better about their abilities at initial response.

4.3.6 Addressing Audit Concerns

While working to achieve her three objectives, Elizabeth has also had to address frequent inquiries concerning the state of BC within the three organizations. These inquiries come from the risk and legal teams involved in the acquisition. Big Money Banks's team is extremely eager to avoid any undue scrutiny from regulators and wishes to ensure that any potential BC problems can be addressed within the consolidated organization before external audits even start. Elizabeth uses her experience following Adaptive BC practices to assure the risk and legal teams' leaders of the legitimacy of her approach. Through her positive relationships with the project team Elizabeth is able to get folks thinking about BC at the beginning of any merger activities. She provides additional guidance to the project team to ensure that gaps or disparities that are identified as part of the merger effort are quickly escalated and proactively dealt with. This demonstrates Elizabeth's competence while the comprehensive metrics developed around departmental and organizational preparedness are expected to satisfy any would-be auditor.

A preliminary audit of the combined organizations is conducted towards the end of the second phase of improvements. As hoped, Elizabeth's reports demonstrating the organization's state of recoverability seem to impress the auditors. They voice some concern around the state of the documented plans but Elizabeth explains, to the auditors' eventual satisfaction, that her objective is to shift focus from documentation to actualized recovery capabilities. She references the survey data from participants and the quantitative measures from the preparedness baseline. She shares the response framework documentation, explaining that the materials are not a script to follow during a crisis, but a reference guide practiced in exercise sessions in order to build muscle-memory and make the process more intuitive should an event occur. Elizabeth's BIA and RA documents largely satisfy the auditors, though she does lose one small battle, as they insist that she go back and categorize the recovery of all services into three tiers. While this will take some additional time in the weeks to come, Elizabeth is certain she can close this finding very quickly.

4.3.7 Outcome

Elizabeth's many quick wins have addressed minor shortcomings but more intensive work will be necessary as the three companies merge. Engagement of the project management office means Elizabeth is now engaged in acquisition activities and can address any BC-related issues proactively. An organized and consistent incident response framework has been implemented meaning events at any of the merging institutions should be escalated and managed effectively. Steps have been taken to address recoverability for critical services. Furthermore, departmental managers are taking ownership for the execution of improvement activities.

Some of the concerns around regulatory support of Elizabeth's approach have been addressed through the preliminary audit. Elizabeth only lost one minor battle around the categorization of services but this should be addressed with little additional effort. Most importantly, Elizabeth's abbreviated BIA and her ability to measure and benchmark the organization's recoverability have demonstrated the value of her approach to those who could most threaten its viability.

At this point, the foundation for the BC program at Big Money Bank has been built and executives informed of the new approach. Support is not unanimous and Elizabeth will likely have to work hard over the coming months to ensure her approach continues to deliver value. Overcoming the expectations that were set by her predecessor have proven a challenge and there are still those in the organization who preferred Chuck's compliance-driven approach. Taking the organization in a new direction will not prove easy and will require time, patience, and work to demonstrate both the existing level of preparedness and the benefits in improved capability that are the result of the Adaptive BC principles and framework.

4.3.8 Lessons Learned

Leadership at Big Money Bank – with its focus on compliance – will be difficult to fully turn around, but it is already starting to change. This is a critical junction for the Adaptive BC framework. Any major regulatory findings or the perception that Elizabeth's program does not measure up to Chuck's could derail the entire effort. At this point, however, some leaders are starting to see value. Continuing to demonstrate the benefits derived from Adaptive BC will be critical to ensure support does not drop and that critics do not have ammunition with which to attack Elizabeth's methods.

No doubt, the identification of significant improvement opportunities has only just begun. At this point, though, Elizabeth has established a reputation for getting things done that will help in future endeavors. By defining the aperture of recovery, Elizabeth has already started to establish the Adaptive BC approach at all three organizations. Her early surveys and discussions to determine preparedness measures and baselines have also set the stage for more comprehensive methods to come. At this point, a rudimentary process exists to ensure visibility should any major disruptions occur. This will need some future attention as areas such as cybersecurity and operations are not yet incorporated into the framework.

From an audit and regulatory perspective, the program seems to be on solid footing. No major concerns have been expressed and there is some early interest in Elizabeth's metrics around organizational preparedness. Defining service-level tiers may prove daunting and this may be one area where the work will have to be incorporated within more value-driven activities. The biggest challenge for Elizabeth will be driving the Adaptive BC approach while still performing some traditional activities in order to satisfy regulators.

4.3.9 Case Study #2: Conclusion

This is called the neo-compliance approach as it demonstrates how a compliance-driven organization can still use Adaptive BC principles to provide value while still satisfying a majority of the expectations of auditors looking for traditional deliverables. As far as providing value, Elizabeth has made monumental improvements in a relatively short period of time. Let's look at a few examples:

- She has improved the response capability within the combined organizations by building a single process within Big Money and informing the appropriate teams within the companies under acquisition to escalate to the appropriate centralized team.
- Through the simple acquisition of 40 laptop bags, Elizabeth has improved the ability of the call center organization to work remotely should an event strike overnight.
- Desktop support has even taken the initiative to address a potential single point of failure within the data center supporting the offshore team.

- The wire transfer recovery process has been formalized within the combined organizations while a long-term solution is in development.
- Recoverability is now a core part of the change management process scope with regards to technology application changes resulting from the impending acquisition.

Elizabeth has satisfied the auditors by being honest and passionate about the direction of the program as well as sharing her metrics and the value they provide. She spent a small amount of time producing the required compliance products, namely the BIA and RA. By quickly getting through these, Elizabeth freed up valuable time to focus on the more important steps in improving overall recoverability. Moving forward, however, Elizabeth realizes that auditors may become increasingly interested in her novel approach to continuity planning, especially her de-emphasis of documentation and recovery time objectives. This may pose a challenge once the acquisition is fully complete, as regulators and auditors are unfamiliar with Adaptive BC and do not know how to effectively review a program following such methods.

4.4 Case Study #3: Taking a Service Centric Approach
4.4.1 GlitzCorp

GlitzCorp is a global media company that started off in the telecommunications industry in the late 1950s. Through organic expansion and acquisition, they now deliver media through multiple channels such as traditional on-air broadcasting, Internet streaming, and mobile platforms. They also produce original content. The company has solid leadership but many parts of the organization operate independently, each with its own unique culture. GlitzCorp is a solid company with a reputable brand but with very disparate views of business continuity depending on which part of the organization one is speaking with.

4.4.2 Meet Gil: GlitzCorp's Director of BC Management

Gil has been brought on as the new director of global business continuity management. This role reports to Rocio, the chief administrative officer. BC responsibilities fall under Rocio's area because the administrative department is responsible for delivering enterprise-level internal services. Rocio's area also includes procurement, corporate travel, safety, security, and facilities. Rocio has asked Gil to pull together the myriad parts of the organization that have BC programs while filling in the gaps where nothing currently exists.

Gil is an experienced business continuity leader. He is very process focused and tackles BC in chunks. Over much of his history, Gil has followed traditional approaches to BC. At his last employer, Gil managed BC but was often at odds with the technology disaster recovery manager over the best way to improve the overall picture at the organization. While the program was considered mature from an industry accepted best practice perspective, Gil often found severe shortcomings. Not wishing to rock the boat and fearful that long-established recovery time objectives might not be met, the technology disaster recovery manager focused an inordinate amount of time and effort preparing for tests and avoiding making significant changes to the program and its documentation even if participants raised concerns. Gil found this to be an untenable state of affairs and, after learning of the Adaptive BC approach from a peer, started following many of the principles outlined in the manifesto. Because of his enthusiasm for Adaptive BC, Gil jumped at the new opportunity at GlitzCorp, as it provided the environment in which he could apply this methodology.

Both Rocio and Gil agree that they should promote and execute BC within GlizCorp as an internal service and not as a governance or compliance activity. Given the variety of maturity levels and exposure to BC in different divisions, he has chosen an approach we dub "service centric." The approach in this scenario focuses on improving recovery capabilities by concentrating on the services within the organization.

4.4.3 Learning the Business

With so many disparate parts of the organization to contend with, Gil decides to set about getting a better understanding of what GlizCorp does and how it does it. He starts with two very basic questions:

- How many buildings do we have and where are they located?
- What departments are in in each building and how do I contact each director?

Much of this information is freely available on the company intranet, so Gil is able to get a good overall feel for the company in a couple of days. Armed with this information, Rocio and Gil spend some time talking about the culture of each of the 37 departments, the personalities of the directors and stakeholders, the kinds of work each department does, and any "landmines" Rocio has experienced while dealing with them in the past. Gil then sets about answering the next two questions as independently as possible:

- What does each department do?
- What BC work has each department done, if any?

Because most directors have dealt with Rocio in the past for centralized administrative services, Rocio sends out an email to each of the 37 directors by name. In it, Rocio asks for information about any BC-related work that has taken place as well as any documentation that exists. Rocio's email gets about a 50% response rate, and Gil splits his time between reading the submitted materials and researching more about each department. At the end of two weeks, Gil has a pretty good idea of the structure of the organization, the willingness of each director to participate in the process, and what BC work has been done to date.

Rocio and Gil decide to start their work with the directors who have been the most responsive or with whom Rocio has the best relationship. Gil schedules a 20-minute introductory meeting with each director, ten in all. Directors are invited to bring additional folks to the meeting as they wish. At the start of each meeting, Gil asks one question: "What is your department all about?" This is a very open-ended question and Gil is a good facilitator of discussion. When appropriate, Gil asks his second question: "What are you, personally, most worried about from the point of view of a potential disaster or significant interruption?" Again, this is an open-ended question designed to see what is foremost on the mind of the director. With this question, Gil learns about each director's worries and "hot button" issues, past experiences with disasters, and possible desires for next steps and priorities.

When the timing is right, Gil asks his final question: "While I've got some ideas about how we can move forward together to further protect your department, what would you like us to do next?"

4.4.4 Delivering Continuous Value While Obtaining Incremental Direction from Leadership

Based on all these interviews, Gil comes up with individual proposals for next steps for each of the ten departments. One department director clearly does not want to take any next steps, so Gil delays working with that department until some future date. Two departments want to start with an exercise, so Gil handles those in accord with the "exercise first" scenario presented in our fifth case study. For the remaining seven departments, Gil sets up a 55-minute kickoff meeting. He leaves it to the director to decide who should attend, but suggests that it be a collection of people who best know the business, operations, and employees of the department. The objectives for these meetings are as follows:

1. Confirm what each department does, including a short description of services and the "owner" or manager of each.
2. Set the "aperture" for planning. This includes the identification of a range of potential losses to plan for and known restrictions for each service.
3. Capture opportunities for improvement.
4. Identify any action items or deliverables, including scheduling the next meeting.

Gil's approach is a discussion-oriented one that provides a great deal of autonomy and grants decision making authority to participants. He makes sure to keep track of any recovery strategy options that come up, as people often jump right into recovery while they are talking about impacts. He also keeps track of any ad hoc issues that are good candidates for next steps to improve his relationship with the group.

Gil spends the next several weeks working with these seven groups at their own speed. Most departments meet once every two weeks for 90 minutes. While at least one representative from each department attends every meeting in order to help shepherd the department through the process, different employees attend different meetings depending on what service is the topic for that meeting. For each service, Gil guides the group to determine the following after they have established loss and restriction constraints (i.e., after they have set the aperture):

- How would we recover this service if ___% of people who are responsible for running this service were unavailable?
- How would we recover this service if ___% of our workspace were unavailable?
- What are the key resources (IT, software, equipment, vital records, etc.) we need to recover this service? What would we do if each of these key resources were unavailable?

After each meeting, Gil documents the results and delivers them back to the department. For each department, he keeps a running list of suggestions for individual improvements, such as procedures to develop, functions to stress in an exercise, or specific resources to obtain. At every step, Gil delivers value to the department and the organization, involving and engaging members along the way.

Once all incident response and service recovery strategies have been determined, Gil sets a baseline for improvement, meeting with each department to measure their capabilities. These measurement sessions accomplish four important things, giving participants:

- A sense of how far they have already come during this brief planning process.
- A sense of how far they have to go to reach a desired preparedness level.
- A specific, quantifiable target for improvement during the next planning effort.
- A feeling of closure as this first planning effort wraps up.

Gil prepares a final deliverable for each department, including an executive summary with capability scores, action items, recommendations for next steps, plans for an exercise, and the quantitative target score for improvement in the next six months. In a short amount of time, Gil and his participants have created a lot of value for the organization and dramatically improved the recovery capabilities of each department.

4.4.5 The Next Phase

Gil and Rocio are seeing a picture emerge that illustrates where individual business operations and departments are in relation to one another. More importantly, a sound incident response process has been established. With regular exercising, participants will build the familiarity and muscle memory to execute should the need arise. Gil has also set some expectations for future work to improve upon existing recovery capabilities. The capability measures from each department help determine where best to focus and Rocio can work with leadership to prioritize the planning effort across all business lines. In the process, Gil has established positive relationships.

Gil and Rocio discuss how to market their results and take next steps with the BC program. They decide on the following steps:

- Obtain permission from the departmental directors to share their *no fault baseline* measures with leadership, set within a context of emphasizing the great work everyone has done to date along with an appendix of specific improvements already made.

No Fault Baseline: Under traditional approaches to business continuity, it is not uncommon for items to be labeled failures or non-compliant, implying fault. The baselines established under Adaptive BC are meant to be "no fault", indicating that the baseline is simply a matter of fact and not the result of the failure of a particular individual, team, or department to perform specific activities.

- Offer an optional and very general lessons learned session for participants from different departments to share their notes with each other.
- Offer an optional business continuity lunch and learn session for the organization, and get a few participants to talk about their experiences with the process.
- Identify the next ten or so departments to work with; have their peers reach out to them and encourage them to join the next "cohort" of BC planners.
- Use positive peer pressure to get other departments to come to the table as well as the competitive aspects of the people and the culture to garner participation.

4.4.6 Outcome

Gil has taken a very detailed, task-oriented approach internally while adopting a conversational and active listening approach with all participants. He has also chosen to work initially with those departments that are most accommodating and willing to participate in the process. This can be used to demonstrate value across the organization, get quick wins, and elicit support from others. For those that have chosen to participate, a significant amount of work has been performed and they are much better prepared as a result. There are, however, 27 more departments that have yet to go through this process. Not only has no work been undertaken on their behalf, but there is still work ahead to define their aperture for recovery as well as establish their level of preparedness.

Gil's approach is an appropriate fit for the department and manager to which he reports. Corporate administration delivers services for the enterprise and BC is no different. Gil provides guidance and support to the departments with which he works but does not manage their activities or make decisions for them. Without governance or compliance requirements to consider or drive the program, Gil is free to work at the pace of each departmental manager and team while demonstrating the benefits of the work they are performing. This initial work will also prove invaluable in proving BC's worth to leadership as preparedness metrics are delivered and comprehensive action plans communicated that demonstrate quantifiable improvement.

The result of all this work will go a long way towards involving the remaining departments in the process:

- The positive results of those who have already participated will help to generate more involvements from others through word of mouth and friendly competition.
- Sharing department-level measures will generate some friendly competition as departments strive to be the "most prepared."
- Sharing the results with leadership will help to establish the legitimacy of the new BC program and begin to set the stage for organizational preparedness as an enterprise-level expectation.
- Measures and baselines can then lead to the establishment of organizational requirements and minimums.

A lot of time and effort has been undertaken to date with much more work ahead. At this point, Gil and his approach have demonstrated their value and set the stage for the larger effort to be done.

4.4.7 Lessons Learned

Gil has benefited from an organization that has not had a BC program and has no regulatory requirements. At the same time, he and his manager have agreed to promote BC as an enterprise service and not a compliance or governance function. This is beneficial in setting a supportive and collaborative atmosphere in which to engage management. Gil grants very explicit authority for decisions and improvement activities to the departments. This gives them some degree of autonomy and responsibility to carry out improvement activities for their own benefit. As a result, Gil has taken a specific path with many of the departments, but also followed different approaches with others based on each manager's direction.

While Gil gained familiarity with Adaptive BC at his previous employer, more experience might have enabled him to expand the scope of his outreach at this juncture. He rightly did not bite off more than he could chew, but he dove deep in each interaction. This has gone a long way in greatly preparing the individual departments he worked with, but a large part of the organization still has no understanding of its level of preparedness and the most difficult work may lie ahead.

Gil was smart in leveraging his manager's existing relationships rather than trying to build his own from scratch. This includes relationships at the executive level which were facilitated by Rocio, freeing Gil to focus on the nuts-and-bolts activities at the department level. At the same time, Rocio performed the initial outreach to directors, greatly speeding the engagement process.

Last, and perhaps most important, the conclusion of this first round has been shared with executive leadership. An expectation has now been set for subsequent deliverables, including the reporting of preparedness measures, improvements performed, next steps, and a gradual increase in scope to eventually encompass the entire organization. No doubt, as leadership becomes familiar with the program and Gil's approach, questions will arise but, for now, the team seems comfortable with actions to date and the path moving forward.

4.4.8 Case Study #3: Conclusion

Because GlitzCorp is not regulated and has not been exposed to traditional BC practices, there are no bad habits to break and no need to try to change minds or take steps to change direction. This also means Gil can enter each discussion with a blank slate. Some discussions are brief and easy, some contentious, and others lengthy and engaging. This drives the individual results of each team.

While detailed, this department-level focus really drives action within the Adaptive BC framework. It also demonstrates that executive committees and up-front buy-in is not a requirement to improve the preparedness picture. Through Gil's example we have also shown that the practitioner need not take a compliance-driven or one-size-fits-all approach to preparedness. By working at each individual department manager's pace, delegating ownership, and providing latitude in identifying improvement opportunities and actions, the practitioner can act as a support member, guiding the process without explicitly owning it.

By focusing on only the departments willing to participate in the process, Gil is able to make meaningful progress without conflict. The end result can then be shared across the organization for the purpose of demonstrating value, engaging others and, eventually, establishing expectations and requirements for the program.

4.5 Case Study #4: Taking a Capabilities-Focused Approach
4.5.1 PeopleMovers Corp

PeopleMovers Corp is a 40-year-old transportation company. It has grown rapidly in the past decade and invested heavily in technology to automate its operations. At the same time, its leadership is young and progressive. The leaders are eager to try new approaches and often pursue the latest trends and buzzwords. The organization has robust emergency management and technology recovery plans – largely because of safety and transportation regulations – but lacks a proper BC program. At the same time, the company's rapid growth means that many critical parts of the organization are underprepared. Senior leaders recognize the need to address preparedness and recoverability but know nothing about the process. Leadership at the organization is young and optimistic but also somewhat naïve.

4.5.2 Meet Leandro: Senior Director of Enterprise Resilience

Leandro has been the disaster recovery manager at PeopleMovers Corp for about a year now. During that time he has reported to the VP of technology service delivery and been focused, almost exclusively, on technology disaster recovery. Over the past year, Leandro has promoted the need for an enterprise-level BC program. As a result, his role has been expanded and his title changed to senior director of enterprise resilience though it still reports to technology service delivery.

Prior to PeopleMovers, Leandro was a junior manager within the enterprise disaster recovery team at a much larger organization. For much of his tenure, Leandro was a dutiful practitioner, participating in the BIA and RA processes and overseeing the development of some 200-plus recovery plans. Over time, Leandro noticed the very rote, almost mechanical, process of BC. The participants he worked with in the business followed suit more to avoid hassles from the compliance and audit departments than from any real desire to build preparedness. In doing research to reignite his passion, Leandro encountered the Adaptive BC Manifesto and quickly found a framework that reflected his own personal feelings about the discipline.

After joining PeopleMovers, Leandro was able to promote the Adaptive BC approach with varying degrees of success. He followed Adaptive BC principles in building the IT department's program but was not able to implement or change things at an enterprise level. With this new expansion of responsibilities, Leandro will finally have the authority to execute this new approach, with little restriction, across the entire organization.

With some parts of the organization well prepared and other parts neglected, Leandro chooses to take measurements in order to do a proper apples-to-apples comparison. He can then use the results to give leadership an illustration of the organization's recoverability and begin to develop priorities for planning purposes. Because Leandro guides each step in line within measures of existing resources, procedures, and competencies, we call this the "capabilities-focused" scenario.

4.5.3 Measure and Benchmark

Leandro has been with the organization for a year and already has the confidence of his management and others within the technology division. Because of this, he chooses not to go to leadership directly. His manager, Kim, has already informed the CIO that Leandro's role has been expanded to include enterprise-level responsibilities and now covers BC, not just IT disaster recovery. Kim and Leandro believe that this alone provides enough justification for Leandro to meet with the appropriate management teams to begin establishing baseline measures and working towards improvement.

Leandro starts by scheduling 30 minutes with each department manager to explain his approach, set some expectations, and enlist their assistance. He also uses this time to define a preliminary aperture of recovery. Following these discussions, Leandro schedules time with each department manager and key members of their respective teams to establish initial metrics. He facilitates a discussion to answer a series of questions meant to build consensus on capabilities. Addressing impacts and not causes of disaster, the questions are based on three basic scenarios:

1. Loss of the primary work location.
2. Loss of staff.
3. Loss of resources.

While working with managers to set the apertures, Leandro learns some pertinent facts that impact the aperture settings. Reservations and ticketing, for example, is very dependent on the availability of employees to answer calls and assist customers. Since the vast majority of call center staff work in one building, unavailability of even a portion of the facility could have a significant impact and must be planned for appropriately. The aperture for loss of staff and work locations is quite low. In the case of safety and security, PeopleMovers employs a geographically diverse staff to provide training, perform audit functions, and work with operational leaders to monitor and improve safety and security within the work environment. Though a critical function, unavailability of even a significant portion of staff does not put customer functions at risk nor does it compromise safety or prevent the departure of vehicles. In this case, the threshold for planning for the loss of staff and work locations is set quite high.

Once armed with the planning aperture, Leandro schedules time with each department. He asks the head of each department to invite as many managers, subject matter experts, and frontline staff as he or she wants, providing that they know enough about the business of the department to provide informed answers. The questions Leandro asks during each department's workgroup meeting follow these general lines:

- In the event your primary workspace – including all onsite hardware and equipment – is lost unexpectedly, approximately what percentage of resources would be immediately available? This includes:
  - Documents and records such as agreements, call lists, and operating procedures.
  - IT devices such as desktops, laptops, phones, and printers.
  - Specialized equipment such as check printers, service equipment, and diagnostic equipment.
  - Supplies such as office letterhead, check stock, and forms.
- In the event of a loss or impact to your primary workspace, to what degree are all the necessary procedures available and known to employees to recover your services? This includes:
  - Assessment of the incident and its impact specifically to your operations.
  - Internal coordination of response activities.
  - Internal communication to employees, management, and leadership.
  - External communication to affected customers, vendors, and stakeholders.
  - Execution of established recovery strategies.
- In the event of a loss or impact to your primary workspace, how competent are management and employees in the execution of response and recovery activities? This includes:

- o The ability to work effectively as a team under stressful circumstances.
- o The fortitude necessary to execute recovery activities and strategies in a post-disaster setting.
- o Demonstrated experience in emergency and disaster response, through exercises, significant threats, or actual events.

Leandro asks the same questions for two additional scenarios: the unavailability of staff and loss of technology systems from an impact to the production data center. While working with departments, he markets this as a "no fault baseline," looking for information with no punishment for low scores. He clearly explains from the outset that future improvements will be measured in terms of growth from the original baseline and that one size does not fit all when it comes to continuously improving capabilities.

Leandro notes that estimations of recovery capabilities can vary quite drastically across his chosen participants. In some cases, respondents have indicated that nothing, or close to it, exists to enable recovery of services. Yet others within the same department rank the availability of resources, procedures, and the competencies of those tasked with recovery extremely high. Leandro contacts all the outliers separately to clarify their responses. In some cases, there is some misinterpretation of the questions and scenarios presented. In others, there is a misunderstanding of what is in place. And in others, there is genuine disagreement about existing capabilities. This information provides Leandro the opportunity to make improvements simply by establishing a consistent understanding of existing recovery capabilities, and facilitating further discussions.

Leandro works through any disparity of understanding by facilitating discussion among participants until everyone is in as close to an agreement as possible regarding preparedness capabilities. Some discussions can get quite heated and Leandro learns that specific teams can be very vocal. In these cases nobody appears easily offended and the team members usually work out their differences in order to come to some mutual understanding. Leandro much prefers intense debate to apathetic silence! It is the meetings in which people are more quiet or conciliatory where Leandro has the most difficulty. In one particular discussion, the department director answers all the questions while everyone else simply nods their agreement. Leandro attempts to challenge what is said and facilitate some discussion but to no avail. Over time, he hopes to build some rapport with the manager in question in order to address some of the more difficult problems.

There are a few instances in which participants do not concede their understanding of recoverability capabilities and some follow-up is necessary to provide evidence as to the existence or lack of specific resources or procedures. Naturally, there are some times where genuine consensus is not possible, and Leandro relies on his experience, expertise, and judgment for a specific measurement.

4.5.4 Continuously Improve Recovery Capabilities

After establishing a baseline, Leandro meets with management to review the results and prioritize the work needed to improve recovery capabilities. It is clear that management appreciates being able to make decisions and to have a significant say in directing the next steps of the BC effort. The management groups work to identify some specific initiatives for the next level of improvements. One of those initiatives involves the reservations and ticketing service, so Leandro gets to work improving the recovery capabilities of this service next.

Reservations and ticketing is a critical department at PeopleMovers. While consumers obtain the vast majority of tickets through the company's online system, there is a centralized call center that exists to take reservations over the phone, answer questions, and address problems and changes not easily resolved through the online tool. Although not critical to keeping vehicles operating, this service is an important part of the company's brand. If call center employees do not resolve issues appropriately, they can escalate quickly, and leadership takes its consumer-friendly reputation very seriously.

Incoming customer calls are handled through two primary channels. A third party with operations offshore runs the first, initial channel. It mostly manages reservation requests and more basic changes and inquiries. This external company has the capacity to quickly expand its services in the event of a sudden increase in demand or in response to a widespread issue, though this capability has never been validated or the process completely vetted. The second channel is a dedicated team within PeopleMovers that handles the more difficult "level two" and "level three" issues. This team primarily operates out of the third floor of the corporate headquarters, but about 25% of the team works from another location in a different city.

Leandro uses this information to paint a picture for leadership of what the customer experience would look like in the event of a loss to locations, people, and resources within the aperture loss settings used for the baseline. Leadership is rightly concerned about the long hold times and inability to effectively address customer issues for a period following an outage. Leandro shares some of the solutions that front-line staff believe could greatly improve recoverability, including:

- Take advantage of the third party's ability to expand capacity within an hour in response to a request from PeopleMovers, made all the more appealing because the third party's operations are located far away from the PeopleMovers call center.
- Triage incoming calls to take advantage of the 25% of PeopleMovers employees who do not work at the corporate headquarters.
- Change existing policies to enable employees to work offsite on a contingency basis.

- Utilize space elsewhere in the corporate headquarters building to seat call center staff should the third floor, specifically, become unavailable.
- Contract for a standby workplace recovery solution that could either be stood up quickly or double as a dedicated offsite conference and meeting location.

Leadership likes the majority of these recommendations. Leandro is instructed to work with the department's management to develop a process to quickly engage the third party and to prove its ability to expand capacity. The PeopleMovers call center director is asked to partner with Leandro to explore the other recommendations. Last, Leandro is asked to obtain cost estimates for a dedicated workspace, though leadership is very clear it is making no promises along these lines.

4.5.5 Outcome

Executive management is impressed with the work to date but Leandro believes they are overly optimistic about what this means for the organization. They are relatively young and unfamiliar with the significant risks they carry. Their concern around the company's very public reputation does mean they take the gaps concerning their call center very seriously. However, they are less concerned about the lack of preparedness for important operational areas that do not directly interact with customers. Leandro will have to keep this in mind as he sets expectations and performs measurements in the near future.

Leadership likes the measurement dashboard and asks Leandro to provide it as a monthly report. Leandro knows that the work to obtain these measures was significant and that a lot of work remains to be done. He asks for a few months to investigate an existing tool to better facilitate the information gathering and reporting process. He also recommends that metrics be provided quarterly instead of monthly until a tool is in place in order to reduce the effort of collecting and collating this data.

Moving forward, Leandro will work with the call center managers to improve their ability to utilize the third party and re-prioritize work in response to an impact to the corporate headquarters. He will also investigate additional options all while facilitating work to improve competencies and develop the procedures to execute these new strategies. More importantly, he will need to work with leadership to identify the next departments for improvement efforts. And all the while, he will need to set expectations with leadership and gently nudge them to look at the less flashy but equally important operational areas of the company.

4.5.6 Lessons Learned

The overly optimistic outlook of executive management needs to be addressed. They believe the few steps taken to date address nearly all their shortcomings. Moving forward, Leandro will have to paint a more robust picture that includes the aperture settings and measurements, including the "no fault baseline" that shows where the organization is overall. This will be important in demonstrating where investment in resources is necessary because of the interrelated nature of resources, procedures, and competencies.

Leandro needs to shore up his measurement process for delivery to leadership at the frequency they have requested. Early on he struggled with how to effectively measure capabilities – in-person meetings, questionnaires, or a combination of both. There was also a lot of follow-up necessary in order to establish some consistency and clear up misinterpretation. Leandro is optimistic but still not certain whether subsequent efforts at measurement will be easier.

Giving department managers the responsibility for picking their priorities and defining recovery strategies and actions for improvement has proven valuable. It is entirely possible that Leandro has taken too big a role in helping establish improvement activities, including bringing options to leadership for decisions. The next iterations may prove daunting as some leaders expect Leandro to "own" BC activities and manage action items.

The no fault baseline has been a great tool for executive management but Leandro should prepare managers that such metrics will be shared while being clear with executive management what these measures mean. Managers don't like surprises and leadership could quickly use this is a compliance tool, requiring completion and improvement on a periodic basis, perhaps as often as monthly. Leandro should be careful not to lose reputational capital with departments that may appear less prepared.

4.5.7 Case Study #4: Conclusion

This is probably the best illustration of the Adaptive BC framework in action with regard to the capabilities and constraint model at its core. Rather than defining objectives without regard for the effort needed to meet them, Leandro started by understanding the current environment. "No fault baseline" measures were taken without the threat of negative consequences. The results of this greatly informed the work of improvement which is the very heart of the Adaptive BC principles.

This is a very action-oriented approach that works best when individual managers are engaged and willing to take responsibility for improvements within their specific areas. The reservations and ticketing example demonstrates the very actionable outcomes of this approach. Clear improvement opportunities and concrete steps to take were identified without the need of a BIA, RA or any of the other overheard associated with traditional approaches.

This is another example in which direct executive approval or engagement is not a necessity. Leandro benefited from his time and experience at PeopleMovers. The trust in his abilities meant he was able to get to work without taking the time in advance to communicate a vision.

In this particular case, the approach Leandro took was suited to the culture at PeopleMovers which has a young and forward-thinking leadership team. As is common, the rapid growth at the company has also resulted in a more open-minded and results-driven mindset. By starting off informally, Leandro was able to build rapport then move to the details of establishing baselines and measurements. This work then informed the resulting actions to improve on recovery capabilities. The next steps in the process were clearly designed to deliver value. The minimal effort to achieve these milestones pleases most managers who are eager to focus on their own primary responsibilities while also still demonstrating improvement in this space.

4.6 Case Study #5: Taking an Exercise First Approach
4.6.1 Stuff2Buy
Stuff2Buy is a well-known retail company that has been in decline and whose reputation has suffered of late. This has left the organization in a bit of turmoil. The company is on its third CEO in the past five years. The previous two each left the company in worse shape than the predecessor after attempting new strategies to turn the company around. The latest top-ranking executive officer has done some significant house cleaning and brought onboard some trusted new members. There is a mix of optimism and distrust in the company. The new leaders inspire confidence and seem to be doing the right things but there is a significant portion of employees who are jaded and distrustful having recently experienced similar upheavals with poor results. The organization has had a BC program for several years, one that followed traditional approaches, but it reflects the high turnover in recent years with little consistency and a lot of documentation that is now very out of date.

4.6.2 Meet Shauna: Vice President of Business Continuity
Shauna was just hired as the VP of business continuity. This is a new role reporting to the chief risk officer (CRO). The new CEO created the CRO role after realizing how little had been done in the risk management space. Both saw a need not just for practical risk management, but for solid preparedness and BC. Their hopes are high not just for the new direction of the company, but for the resilience anticipated from this renewed focus.

For almost her entire twenty years in the discipline, Shauna followed traditional practices. For much of that time she felt confident in her ability to execute against industry accepted best practices and felt her program resulted in a highly prepared organization. An event at her most recent employer opened her eyes to just how unprepared they were. Businesses that had detailed recovery plans attempted to follow them but with poor results. In an attempt to revamp the program at her manager's request Shauna learned of the Adaptive BC manifesto. She learned of a peer at another organization following Adaptive BC principles and of that individual's success in generating value with fewer resources and in shorter timeframes. While familiar with the approach, her own experience in executing such an approach is limited. Her new role at Stuff2Buy will prove to be enlightening.

Shauna has chosen to use an "exercise first" approach in order to build engagement and produce quick wins to propel the program forward. Shauna is an action-oriented, roll-up-her-sleeves type, and exercises provide an opportunity to quickly get her hands dirty. She is also very detail oriented and the data she gleans from exercises paired with her focus on detailing departmental services will help provide valuable improvements.

4.6.3 Setting the Stage

Shauna deliberately decides not to engage executive leadership at this time. She knows from what she has learned so far of Adaptive BC that executive engagement is not a necessary component of building preparedness capability. Shauna has also learned that the primary responsibility of leadership is to return the organization to profitability. This will require a serious focus on cutting costs and realizing efficiencies while evaluating the products and services that are the highest priority. Engaging the executive level with regard to BC might actually damage her credibility; developing some ground-level capability will have much greater impact in the short-term. Shauna reports to the CRO and has already informed him of her approach. He is supportive of her desire to focus on delivering value rather than spending time trying to outline a vision for executive buy-in.

Before starting, Shauna checks in with a few members of the senior HR team. She recognizes that exercises can go a long way towards achieving some objectives that are important from an HR standpoint. For one thing, exercises are a great way to help build teams. For another, exercises are good leadership training, especially for those individuals the organization is grooming for more senior positions. Making decisions with limited information, motivating people towards a common objective, and taking charge of a chaotic situation are all activities that directly relate to leadership development. Furthermore, exercises help people to experience different decision-making, management, and personality styles, especially those styles that reveal themselves best under stress.

4.6.4 Starting with Capabilities

In terms of preparedness capabilities and organizational culture, the departments at Stuff2Buy cover a very wide spectrum. Shauna believes that the best way to engage people is through exercises. She starts big by conducting some rather large tabletops with multiple layers of management. This provides some interesting results as well as some great learning opportunities. After some deep dives, Shauna learns that one of the most critical issues is the lack of a process to report and escalate events once they occur. In some cases, even relatively minor disruptions have resulted in significant impacts. The most recent issue was a power outage that went unresolved for nearly two days.

Shauna next conducts a few small exercises directly with retail location participants. In some cases, she tries a format she calls the "instant exercise." She has the participants roll dice to randomly determine external conditions like the day of the week, time of day, and weather. She then has a participant randomly pick one of several different scenarios that detail the unavailability of locations, staff, or resources in some particular way. There are no "smoking hole" scenarios. In all cases, the scenarios are fairly mundane, such as system and power outages, snowstorms, and street flooding. Because Shauna's approach is fun and includes aspects of gamification, randomization, and realistic scenarios, most groups are very responsive.

In her exercises with support teams, Shauna learns of the many different documents and written procedures that exist to facilitate manual work at the retail branch level. Support team members have a wealth of knowledge and experience enabling such work and are able to guide local managers in response and recovery activities. It becomes apparent that no investment has been made in BC beyond writing a handful of incident response procedures. Looking at the documentation, Shauna determines that much of it is predicated on having specific resources that are not, in fact, available. Whether the procurement of such resources was planned or if there were just a lot of poorly made assumptions, Shauna is not sure. Regardless, the picture of recovery at the retail level is fairly poor though many opportunities exist to quickly improve.

The picture at corporate headquarters is even worse. Very little exists in terms of resources or procedures for critical support teams, including the call center, finance, HR, and technology. The exercises that Shauna conducts with each of these departments provides some great insight regarding the relative competencies of those in charge. Finance, in particular, has a great deal of interest in preparation activities. They have detailed procedures but exercises reveal their ineffectiveness and some drastic disparity in competencies across the management team. The call center and technology teams, by contrast, have little in the way of documented procedures but leadership of both areas is experienced in dealing with disasters.

The good news is that the exercises reveal a willingness to close existing gaps across many of the departments. They also provide great benefit in the form of identifying what current capabilities exist. Even without current procedures, robust competencies, or a formal program, managers and staff alike have a sense of urgency around potential incidents and many reveal a willingness to step in and take action should the need arise. In many exercises, Shauna does not even need to facilitate or guide participants. Many of them, through open dialog, reveal their response instincts, which in turn informs other participants, generating further meaningful discussion. Simply discussing the response without the stress of having an actual incident helps raise awareness, a step toward better preparedness. The results are extremely meaningful as groups identify shortcomings and, in some cases, create and assign action items.

4.6.5 Achieving Rapid Results in Iterations
The results of the initial exercises translate into some quick wins in finance and operations. Finance, in particular, discovers that the department's recovery procedures rely heavily on the existence of remote resources that, in current reality, simply do not

exist. The exercise also reveals a number of single-point failure modes within the operations environment. After some discussion, several workarounds are identified, and a number of individuals volunteer to help update the corresponding procedures.

Human resources, by contrast, is extremely disengaged. Management focuses on irrelevant details, while HR staff members try to deflect responsibility and downplay the critical nature of the work they do, such as the delivery of paychecks and benefits.

While it is a daunting thought, Shauna realizes that the "biggest bang for the buck" will be found in improvements that can be created, scaled, and rolled out to large numbers of retail locations. With over 100 retail locations to consider nationwide, this will be a big challenge, but it is where the greatest improvement can be realized the fastest and at relatively little cost.

She begins by thinking specifically about recovery resources. She knows that boosting operational profitability is of paramount concern and that there is no stomach for investment in duplicate resources for recovery purposes. So Shauna limits her focus to getting the most out of existing resources without requiring the purchase of additional items. From there she works with the appropriate teams to determine if equipment exists that can be redistributed to locations in greater need and if any such resources require maintenance or repair. Surprisingly she finds some locations with nothing by way of laptops, printers, or other critical technical equipment while other locations have a surplus. It is a very straightforward process to properly redistribute these standard recovery resources across the retail locations. Shipping and reconfiguring these items will incur some cost and effort but it is minimal and the CRO easily approves funding of the effort.

While redistribution of resources is underway, Shauna works with the centralized safety, security, facilities, technology, and operational support team members to develop general procedures for retail locations. They also create a process to rapidly assemble by phone in the event of any disruption to a retail location's operations. Shauna exercises this process with the new response team on a Tuesday only to be faced with an actual event the following Thursday. While the team assembled quickly, Thursday's actual response conference call was poorly coordinated and chaotic. Team members spoke over one another attempting to determine the impact to their respective areas while trying to provide guidance. Learning from these lessons, Shauna created a call facilitator role and developed a prioritized checklist for the team to walk through. The response team exercised this process just over a week later.

Shauna determines that providing direct guidance to each of the 100-plus retail locations would be beneficial, but far from practical. Leveraging some of the relationship capital she has gained to date, she works with the marketing department to create an easily digestible playbook for retail stores. Because she wants to know how these playbooks will be received and then used in real life, she decides to perform a few experiments. She facilitates exercises at three representative locations. In these sessions, Shauna gets as much perspective and input as possible. She then goes back to some of the corporate support teams such as security and technology to discuss what she learned and some of the specific concerns that the stores raised. At one point, Shauna even arranges a two-hour discussion with one retail location to review their feedback with the entire corporate response team and senior IT support staff. This turns out to be a constructive meeting in which proper expectations are set with the local retail team members. It also proves very informative to the support folks who get to learn about the unique challenges faced at the retail level. Shauna refines the playbook and seeks support, once again, from corporate marketing to help distribute and promote it.

4.6.6 Tackling Challenges

The focus on improving the state of the retail locations has meant that corporate support functions have received less attention. Exercises with these departments generated a lot of early enthusiasm but Shauna has been unable to stay on top of all the work needed to improve these areas. She was able to get management teams to take some responsibility, in finance and technology at least, so not all the momentum has been lost. The call center took some early steps to improve its recovery capabilities but has not taken any significant action since. Human resources, as Shauna expected, has not made any changes and does not appear interested in doing so.

Shauna intends to take the results of her most recent exercises to develop some rudimentary metrics. She also lists the specific advancements made in each area and the next actions needed to further improve. She shares all of this with the CRO for presentation to leadership in an upcoming risk meeting. She reaches out to the operations teams and support function managers to inform them that these details will be shared with executives in the coming weeks. The director of the call center, William, contacts Shauna directly with concerns about how the lack of effort will be perceived by leadership. Shauna responds honestly that she does not know how these details will be received and what, if any, concerns or actions will come down from the executive team after learning these details. She does encourage William to take steps towards addressing the call center's recoverability since improvement, not maintaining current capabilities, will be objectives of the program and highlighted in future reports.

4.6.6 Outcome

Given the turmoil that has existed at Stuff2Buy over recent years, Shauna's exercises provide a much-needed respite for employees dealing with constant changes and cutbacks. At the same time, the involvement of managers and staff in these activities provides them common objectives on which to collaborate. The further engagement of support team members also demonstrates to ground-level staff and teams in remote retail locations that resources exist to help them and that individuals are willing and eager to assist. In many cases, this is the first time these groups have worked together, and many begin to work together regularly on other mutually-beneficial activities. This goes a long way towards changing some negative attitudes that had developed from the years of struggles with profitability and the turmoil at the leadership level.

While significantly more work is needed, Shauna has made major strides in improving recovery capabilities for Stuff2Buy. Not even a month after the roll-out of the playbook another event occurs in one of the larger markets. The response team demonstrates marked improvement in its ability to collaborate effectively in support of the impacted location.

Moving forward, Shauna intends to use the work she has done to build more momentum and demonstrate to management what can be accomplished in a relatively short period. She hopes that in the coming months this will be enough to convince executives to make the necessary investment in resources needed to improve recoverability at the retail level. In the meantime, she will use the results of any future events as well as the input of the response team as solid evidence that the changes made are having the intended benefits. She is also working with security to document past and future losses following disruptions that affect retail locations in order to demonstrate the value BC is providing to the organization and how it contributes to overall profitability.

4.6.7 Lessons Learned

Shauna's approach has significantly improved the state of the retail environment in a relatively short period and for relatively little cost. Not only from a preparedness perspective, but by bringing teams together she has managed to improve attitudes and foster greater collaboration. No doubt some changes will be needed to improve performance and efficiency at the retail level. As such investments are made to the retail and corporate operations, Shauna will need to ensure she is engaged so recoverability is a consideration and does not interfere or put preparedness as risk. Her biggest challenge will be to capitalize on her early wins while not stretching herself too thin by expanding the scope of what she can reasonably accomplish in her BC program.

One of the biggest benefits of this approach is the rapid improvement in crisis competencies, a frequently overlooked component of robust recoverability. Enhancing the proficiency of leaders to effectively manage through a crisis sometimes has the greatest impact on overall recoverability, with the lowest capital investment. The drawback to such a focus is that other aspects of recoverability, such as procedures and resources, may receive less attention and lower investment as management seeks to improve for the lowest possible cost.

At this point, it is easy to get into a cadence of regular exercising with less attention paid to the interim work. Shauna will need to focus as much, or perhaps more, effort on the action steps needed to improve recovery capabilities. There is also the risk that attention and engagement will wane as exercises become a periodic activity or as participants become too familiar with the process and stop thinking creatively about response and recovery.

4.6.8 Case Study #5: Conclusion

The exercise-first approach has proven effective at Stuff2Buy for a number of reasons. Shauna has successfully eliminated a large portion of the upfront work dictated by traditional approaches to BC, including:

- Obtaining executive buy-in and support from the start of the process.
- Performing a BIA and RA.
- Developing extensive plans.
- Developing response around worst-case scenarios (the proverbial "smoking hole").

At the same time, Shauna has managed to focus on process, not documentation. Exercises have gone a long way towards informing Shauna, the department managers, and, ultimately, executive management, about the state of preparedness at Stuff2Buy. This information has been used to identify specific steps that can improve overall recoverability. Let's look at some of the other advantages of this approach:

- Rather than developing procedures separately for training and education later on, Shauna has developed a process that more closely follows what managers and team members would do intuitively.
- Exercises have reinforced the understanding that exists across the operations and support teams while also providing evidence of the need for necessary changes that can have a large impact.
- Conducting multiple, varied exercises enables participants to walk through a wider variety of scenarios in greater details, thereby providing a great deal of information about existing capabilities and opportunities for improvement.
- Exercises are a far more engaging process than surveys and analysis. Shauna has even managed to improve the overall culture at Stuff2Buy through the process.

Using exercises, Shauna has managed to engage a large number of peers and managers. The effort has improved capabilities for those who participated while painting a meaningful picture of the state of recoverability. This data has also been used to deliver initial measurements to the leadership team via the CRO. Sharing the metrics data prior to distribution has also garnered some interest from teams that had previously been disengaged. In short, this approach has maximized engagement and highlighted some of the gaps that exist in organizational preparedness: namely, the lack of crisis competencies that could negatively impact response and recovery efforts. The results have brought disparate teams together and greatly improved the recovery capabilities picture where it matters most: at Stuff2Buy's retail locations.

4.7 Transition

This chapter is meant to provide five examples only, and is by no means comprehensive. We believe we have provided a fuller picture of what Adaptive BC looks like in execution, explaining the overall processes and the many ways of executing the framework, along with some specific examples thrown in to illustrate the good and the bad. The BC protagonists in these examples probably met with somewhat more success than they might have in real life, but naturally we wanted the good guys to win. Our experience, and that of our peers who are already executing BC in new and innovative ways, is that these techniques actually do deliver greater benefits with less effort and greater engagement.

As a side note, while setting and readjusting the aperture is a core component of Adaptive BC, there have been sections of this chapter in which this was not mentioned. This is not to imply that setting the aperture is unnecessary, but that it may be a lower priority in some circumstances. In some environments, it will make sense to start by setting the aperture with either executive leadership or with departmental managers. In other cases, the challenges and opportunities for improvement will be obvious, making the aperture less critical until such issues have been adequately addressed. Regardless of the situation, it is an essential component to keep in mind.

Having worked our way through a foundation in Chapter 2, specific steps in Chapter 3, and a handful of examples in Chapter 4, we now turn our attention to Chapter 5 where we examine some influences from related disciplines and the lessons they have to share with us for the practice of Adaptive BC. We then look at the place of Adaptive BC within the industry, think about some potential far-reaching consequences, and provide some final thoughts about innovation and creativity.

Chapter 5

Dwelling

"Dwelling is not primarily inhabiting but taking care of and creating that space within which something comes into its own and flourishes." – Martin Heidegger's *Building, Dwelling, Thinking*

In this final chapter, we take a closer look at the nature of Adaptive Business Continuity (Adaptive BC) planning and consider what it might be like to dwell in the new space that this framework provides. Adaptive BC planning itself did not begin from scratch – it builds upon improvements from inside and outside the profession. We'll spend some time discussing lessons learned from related disciplines, explore a little more about the nonlinear and sometimes paradoxical nature of Adaptive BC, and then look to the future of our industry and how it might relate to a new adaptive planning paradigm. We hope this chapter will encourage you to find a space for Adaptive BC in your own career as we work together to find a space for it within the industry.

This chapter will help you to:

- Adopt lessons learned from related disciplines like project management and lean process improvement.
- Further improve your application of Adaptive BC practices.
- Gain a deeper understanding of the iterative and nonlinear nature of Adaptive BC practices.
- Explore the possibilities of a new kind of academic approach to business continuity (BC) training.
- Consider the past and possible future of Adaptive BC practices within the industry.
- Be motivated to try Adaptive BC practices in your organization.

5.1 Dwelling in the Adaptive BC House

What would it be like to dwell in this Adaptive BC "house" that we are building, and how does it fit into the rest of the "neighborhood"? In this final chapter of the book, we look at adopting the Adaptive BC approach in your practice and in our industry.

There are two important concepts for this book's final chapter:

- First, we have attempted to create a "space," as Martin Heidegger might call it, specifically for BC. We have delineated BC from other professions such as crisis management, emergency management, and risk management. While the typical BC practitioner often has responsibilities in all these related fields, it is important to demarcate each as a separate discipline. While many published guides attempt to merge these subjects, we find that few clearly define BC as a distinct discipline. If BC is going to mature, it must have a proper delineation of what is, and is not, included in its body of knowledge. We have also carved out a new space for an Adaptive BC approach that is separate from traditional BC practices.

- Second, it should be clear by now that the Adaptive BC approach is nonlinear. This is not accidental. As we discuss below, a consistent feedback mechanism to provide value while simultaneously learning from the customer is a hallmark of innovations in project management, lean process improvement, and other disciplines. No BC program ever starts from scratch; there are always pre-existing competencies within the organization upon which to improve. With each deliverable, the practitioner learns more about the business and the needs of the customer, continuing to refine the next deliverable to produce more value. In fact, it may be that the practitioner and the participants only fully come to an understanding of what needs to be done after they have been working together for some time. The Adaptive BC approach is also nonlinear in that you can begin anywhere within the aperture, the program, or the capabilities, and then move on to anywhere else. One size does not fit all, and while it is possible to provide a theoretical foundation for your work, a framework for your practice, and a finishing of examples to emulate, it is ill advised to suggest specific sequential instructions. You must tailor each step of the Adaptive BC program to match the culture of the organization, with its specific situations and individuals.
Remember, you are building a mutually beneficial partnership that will last a long time.

We have divided this chapter into the following six sections:
1. Learning Lessons from Lean, Agile, and Project Management 2.0.
2. The Great Gestalt Switch.
3. The Paradox of the Paradigm's Practitioners.
4. Advice and Appeals to Auditors.
5. Forecasting the Future.
6. Closing: Creative Continuity Planning.

5.2 Learning Lessons from Lean, Agile, and Project Management 2.0

The Adaptive BC framework was not formed in a vacuum. Many thought leaders have pointed out specific problems within traditional continuity planning that need to be overcome and many planners have shared new practices that have proven beneficial. While these advances within our own discipline are important, equally important are some of the large-scale changes that have taken place within disciplines that intersect with BC.

Fields related to BC have undergone substantial transformations. Leadership, business, general management, project management, training, education, and others have undergone significant advances in methodology and technique in just a few decades. Technology has played a large role in many, though not all, of these advancements. Needless to say, operating in a global economy has changed a great deal since the advent of mainframe computing.

In this section, we will briefly survey advances from other fields that have been and can be brought to bear on Adaptive BC. In particular, we will focus on innovations within project management and lean process improvement. This does not represent a comprehensive look at all changes within these two fields, nor is it an attempt to identify all influencers of Adaptive BC. We are simply calling out the ideas and practices from other disciplines that helped shape the approaches outlined in this book. In this way, we hope that this will provide a greater context for understanding the approach and implementing the Adaptive BC framework in your BC programs.

5.2.1 Traditional Project Management

We believe that project management offers important insights into our own discipline. Several years ago, critics of formalized project management practices raised complaints comparable to the ones we hear today about BC, namely that it contains too much "overhead" and takes time away from the "real work" of an organization. Project management was not considered a profession, and practitioners were not recognized for their unique skillset.

Spearheaded largely by the Project Management Institute (PMI), thought-leaders in the field fought back through research and publications. The PMI took pains to prove that formal project management techniques improved the success of projects across the board and provided benefits according to any measure: customer satisfaction, employee satisfaction, project budget performance, reduction of rework, return on investment, time to market, and so forth. The PMI also made sure to publicize these results, marketing to practitioners, leaders, and executives. Project management is now widely recognized as a profession in its own right, and its practitioners as professionals.

We highlight the project management profession for three reasons. First, we believe that research as to the demonstrable and measurable effectiveness of a formal BC program could go a long way to enhancing the recognition of our discipline as a profession and our practitioners as professionals. Support organizations, research centers, and academic institutions would be wise to follow the path set by the PMI to fund such research and invest in marketing its results. Second, though they may not recognize it, continuity practitioners pull a great deal of their program work from project management. Many activities involved in the creation and execution of a BC program stem from best practices within project management. Third, note that traditional project management evolved over time. The original guide to the Project Management Body of Knowledge (PMBOK) was less than two hundred pages when first published in 1996; yet, by the time the fifth edition was published in 2013, the subject had matured to the point that this edition was nearly 600 pages long.

Interestingly, project management not only evolved and improved along the established principles inherent within its theory, but eventually something unexpected happened. An entirely new approach to project management developed on its own as an alternate to the traditional approach: Agile project management.

5.2.2 Agile Project Management

Agile project management, also called "agile software development" or just "Agile," got its official start in 2001 and is continuing to mature. Agile arose as a response to the following two significant challenges inherent in software development:

- The practical inability to accurately define all requirements upfront.
- The practical inability to accurately forecast when the full design, development, testing, and launch efforts would finish.

Because of the many problems inherent in finalizing the requirements before beginning design and development work, Agile rejected the traditional belief that all requirements had to be defined as the first step in creating software. Instead, Agile projects begin with a general understanding of what the software needs to do then generate detailed requirements along the way. While Agile team members do make calculated guesses as to when sets of related functionality will be ready to ship, they do not try to predict when an entire system will be completed.

Software is usually created in two- to four-week iterations called "sprints." At the beginning of each sprint, the project team works with the customer to determine what functionality will be delivered at the end of the sprint. The team partners closely with customers and stakeholders throughout the life of the entire initiative to ensure that everyone understands the progress towards the desired outcomes. At the end of most sprints, the team delivers new, fully operational functionality in the software. This is a fast-paced process whereby the customer continuously takes delivery of workable software after a few weeks or months of time while the project learns more and more about what the customer finds valuable. Transparency and productive feedback are built directly into the Agile process.

Here are the takeaways from Agile that you can easily adopt for your Adaptive BC program:

- **Work in short iterations.** The Adaptive BC planner should provide benefit and value in a matter of days and weeks, not months and years. He or she should work in very short iterations ("sprints") to produce deliverables.
- **Deliver continuous value.** The planner should deliver valuable outcomes to the customer every step of the way. Whether it be an updated procedure, an improved competency, or a new physical resource, the planner can identify the deliverable and help provide it in short order. Each short iteration should result in a deliverable that provides a benefit in line with the needs of the customer and the business objectives of the organization. The wise practitioner is both theoretically and realistically able to walk away from the engagement at the end of any given iteration if needed and still leave the customer with usable deliverables.
- **Partner closely with all stakeholders.** What should we do first? What are the highest priorities? Where are the biggest benefits? Planners do not answer these questions; customers do. It is a central mission of the practitioner to partner closely with everyone involved in this process to ensure transparency and value, balancing the needs of the organization, the department, and the BC program.
- **Remain adaptive.** As stakeholders learn more about the nature of continuity planning and the benefits it can provide, they may change their minds about deliverables and next steps. This is to be expected and embraced. The practitioner should adapt to the needs of every department, adjusting to the business, culture, personality, and other drivers that differentiate one department from another. The customer may not know what they want or need at the beginning of this process, but as he or she learns the process and better understands what is needed, the practitioner should quickly adapt.

5.2.3 Project Management 2.0

Before leaving the topic of project management, we should briefly note another new trend in that field. Dr. Harold Kerzner, a key figure and thought leader in the project management discipline, released a book in 2015 that presented the next evolution in his thinking. Calling his new approach "Project Management 2.0," Dr. Kerzner notes that today's projects must operate in an environment "where politics, risk, value, company image and reputation, goodwill, sustainability, and quality are seen as being potentially more important to the firm than the traditional time, cost, and scope constraints" and, "as such, the traditional project management practices that we have used for decades… are now seen as ineffective….” (p. 1). Project managers must focus on delivering value with the work they perform, developing their business acumen to succeed despite a myriad of conflicting constraints.

Three of the main tenants of Project Management 2.0 (PM 2.0) are as follows:
- Deliver value.
- Customize methodology to meet client needs.
- Use metrics within dashboards.

5.2.3.1 Deliver Value
What good is delivering something that no one wants? Project managers have traditionally considered their projects successful if they came in on time, within budget, and within scope. But there is the growing recognition that what determines success is whether the deliverables were able to provide the benefits expected by the customer. A project may finish on time, within budget, and within scope and still be a failure because the customer was not provided with meaningful benefits. If work does not generate value for the customer and the parent organization, it cannot be considered a success.

Similarly, BC practitioners have considered their planning a success if it was performed while following recommended standards and practices. If you deliver a business impact analysis (BIA) and risk assessment (RA) document within the timeframe you promised, you must have succeeded. Not so if you cannot translate these documents into something of benefit to the business. “An essential success criterion with PM 2.0 is that projects must provide some degree of value when completed…” (Kerzner, 2015, p.53).

5.2.3.2 Customize Methodology to Meet Client Needs
One size does not meet all. This is as true in project management as it is in BC planning. As Kerzner summarizes, “…you may need to develop a different project management methodology or apply your existing methodology differently to interface with each stakeholder given that each stakeholder may have different requirements and expectations and most complex projects have long time spans” (Kerzner, 2015, p.32). Because value is understood in terms of benefits, and benefits are specific to the particular makeup and environment of the customer, the professional will to have to adjust his or her methodology to meet customer needs. As Kerzner explains, “The project manager will walk through a cafeteria and select… those elements/activities that best fit a particular project. At the end of the cafeteria line, the project manager, accompanied by the project team, will combine all of the elements/activities into a project playbook specifically designed for a particular client” (p.5).

Likewise, the Adaptive BC practitioner must be aware of the specific needs of his or her customer and the specific culture of the customer’s organization. The practitioner takes advantage of a responsive framework instead of a linear methodology. He or she inventories the different tools at his or her disposal, and chooses the types and order of techniques that will offer the most value while continuously improving recoverability capabilities. The result is an adaptive playbook specifically designed to maximize the recoverability of a particular client within all known constraints. Imagine the powerful combination of an Adaptive BC approach, customized playbook, and response portfolio delivered in quick iterations to the organization!

5.2.3.3 Use Metrics Within Dashboards

We all know that people, and especially executives, respond better to images than to words on a page. Kerzner maintains that managers of PM 2.0 need to provide information to stakeholders in terms of dashboards: "Executives and customers desire a visual display of the most critical… information in the least amount of space" (Kerzner, 2015, p.5). No one wants a 30-page document when a single image will suffice. We all are much more attracted to infographics than text, and we are getting better at creating and interpreting such images. Customers will be receptive to dashboards that are customized just for them and provide just the information they care about.

But what metrics do we include in these dashboards? For project management, these metrics are key performance indicators (KPIs) that speak to the health of the project as it operates within a set of constraints. For the Adaptive BC practitioner, these metrics are the resources, procedures, and competencies that make up the measurable recoverability capabilities of the organization, along with the aperture that sets the scope for these capabilities. "If you cannot offer a stakeholder something that can be measured, then how can you promise that their expectations will be met? You cannot control what you cannot measure" (p.79). The Adaptive practitioner sets the aperture that identifies the constraints for the organization, measures existing capabilities, and then reports these metrics as visual indicators on a dashboard. The dashboard informs your stakeholders, helping them to make data-driven decisions to move forward with the next iteration in the continuous capability improvement cycle.

5.2.4 Lean Process Improvement

One can find many different definitions, models, and practices under the broad banner of *lean*. The following explanation from Lean Enterprise Institute (n.d.) suffices for our discussion:

> Simply, lean means creating more value for customers with fewer resources.
> A lean organization understands customer value and focuses its key processes
> to continuously increase it. The ultimate goal is to provide perfect value to the
> customer through a perfect value creation process that has zero waste….
> Companies are able to respond to changing customer desires with high
> variety, high quality, low cost, and with very fast throughput times.

Within the lean movement, we see familiar themes from Agile, namely a customer-centric focus on value with rapid and flexible cycles to create usable deliverables. Like the Adaptive BC approach, lean "…is not a tactic or a cost reduction program, but a way of thinking and acting for an entire organization" (Lean Enterprise Institute, n.d.).

While there are a great deal of proven practices, recommendations, tools, and techniques that now constitute the evolving lean approach, for our purposes, we can focus on just three important themes. In the past few years, themes like these three have become part of the vocabulary of business and have been used widely in popular business books to describe basic trends that relate to lean process improvement adopted and adapted in a wide variety of situations, industries, and organizations:

- Deliver the minimum viable product.
- Fail fast.
- Stay flexible and be ready to pivot.

5.2.4.1 Deliver the Minimum Viable Product

A minimum viable product (MVP) is a pared-down deliverable with enough functionality to satisfy the customer with regard to some portion of the value he or she is seeking. The team learns about additional requirements and expectations from the customer's reaction to each delivery of the product. In short, an MVP is the smallest thing you can deliver to the customer that satisfies a requirement and that informs you of next steps for improvement. The MVP must be usable and valuable to the customer. In the software industry, MVP is a small collection of features that provides the customer some desired functionality and lets developers know how to respond with the next feature set. In the manufacturing world, this is a low investment, quickly produced, standalone product that satisfies a demand and informs designers of how to shape the next version. In BC, an MVP is a rapidly produced deliverable that increases the recovery capabilities of an organization while providing feedback to the planner on the next step for continuous improvement of those capabilities.

5.2.4.2 Fail Fast

It would be foolish to spend a long time creating a product that no one wanted. But that is just what happens with many software development teams. This also happens with too many of our traditional continuity planning efforts; when is the last time anyone was delighted to receive a 50-page business impact analysis document after six months of work? Ideally, you should produce small deliverables that provide large value with minimal work. By so doing, you learn what is important within your organization and what is not. You learn what is valued within your customer's culture and what is not. By failing fast, you are able to make early course corrections in your work with each area of the organization. Business acumen will be critical to your ongoing success.

5.2.4.3 Stay Flexible and Be Ready to Pivot

Based on what you learn from your small and rapid deliverables, you may have to pivot and change your approach. Pivoting allows you to focus on what is most important to the customer. If recovery strategy development is meeting with resistance, pivot to focus on the vice president's hot button issues. If motivation seems low, try running an exercise. Just like a startup must sometimes make significant changes in its product offerings in order to ensure continued marketplace share, so too must the Adaptive BC planner be ready to change his or her tactics to maximize value.

Lean has influenced many different disciplines making them more effective and efficient. To date, traditional continuity planning has absorbed and incorporated very little from lean. But the Adaptive BC approach integrates much of the lean philosophy in the core of its framework. The Adaptive BC planner can gain a great advantage by shifting his or her thinking to a paradigm that allows him or her to "respond to changing customer desires with high variety, high quality, low cost, and with very fast throughput times" (Lean Enterprise Institute, n.d.).

5.3 The Great Gestalt Switch

Gestalt switch is a term you don't hear very often. The gestalt switch, or gestalt shift as it is also known, occurs when your entire perception of something changes. Figure 5-1 is a classic example. It is an image of either an old woman or a young woman depending on how you see it.

Figure 5-1. Woman Gestalt Example (https://s-media-cache-ak0.pinimg.com/564x/e6/d5/37/e6d5376649f288f8d06ef8bc73d7e7a5.jpg)

In some cases, making the shift between one image and another is easy. Other times we instantly spot one image but struggle to undo what we perceive in order to see something else. The same goes for ideas and concepts. Most of us have been there at one time or another – that "ah-ha moment" when the light bulb goes on and we suddenly understand something we've struggled with for some time. The difficulty stems from trying to view the new paradigm from the vantage point of the old one.

5.3.1 The Traditional BC Perspective

In terms of Adaptive BC, we have noticed some interesting reactions when practitioners are exposed to this new approach for the first time. When Adaptive BC principles are evaluated independently of one another, we can see how many practitioners could take issue with individual changes we have proposed. But these components are only part of a comprehensive framework. For example, in traditional BC, eliminating the BIA does not make any sense. Just about everything within the old approach revolves around or is directly dependent on the BIA and its results. Adaptive BC seeks to define a new approach in which both the process of the BIA, as well as its deliverables, are completely unnecessary.

Traditional BC planning is somewhat linear. By contrast, Adaptive BC is more holistic. The old methods and standards dictate what must be done and, to a certain degree, how and when it is done. There is an ordered progression of activities. But Adaptive BC seeks to change that paradigm by applying principles to the entire effort. In essence, the principles apply no matter what activity you happen to be performing. If you are exercising your program it is important to deliver continuous value, engage at many levels of the organization, and use documentation as appropriate and not as a driver of execution.

5.3.2 A Change in Objectives

Consider also that traditional BC seeks to define processes for managing a business continuity program or system. Adaptive BC seeks to define a framework for preparing organizations to continue business in the event of a disruption. It is a rather subtle difference but the ramifications are significant. This changes the focus from how to effectively manage the teams and mechanisms of a BC program to how businesses can be better prepared. One can argue that the objective of any BC management system is to better prepare an organization. That is true, but traditional BC speaks to how an individual or team executes the steps to prepare an organization while providing little to ensure that those steps are done to the greatest advantage. Traditional BC is internally focused on the execution of activities and the delivery of materials. Adaptive BC focuses on the organization and how improvements are made for its benefit. Coupled with the consistent application of all principles, this makes the Adaptive BC effort more effective and moves us closer to doing the right things in the right way rather than just doing things because the practice guide says to. The difference is subtle, but we believe it represents a wholesale change of perspective. In his 1962 classic, *The Structure of Scientific Revolutions*, Thomas Kuhn, one of the great contributors to Gestalt psychology, created the term "paradigm shift." Kuhn wrote, "Paradigm shifts do not occur because of a single convincing argument. Rather, different arguments convince different scientists."

5.3.3 The Whole Is Greater Than Its Parts

An important concept within Gestalt psychology is the idea that the whole is greater than the sum of its parts. While this means different things in different fields, for Adaptive BC we take it to mean that no particular activity or set of activities is indispensable in achieving BC objectives; rather, the entire collection taken together constitutes the proper approach to continuity planning. Think back again to the image of the young/old woman in Figure 5-1. It is not important that you see a mouth compared to a neck, or an ear instead of an eye. What is important is that an entire image appears to you all at once and all together. You do not discern a particular feature, like an ear, but the whole of the image. So too with Adaptive BC – it is helpful to think of the approach as a whole, not a collection of individual activities. Individual activities are far less important than the organizing objective of the continuous improvement of measurable recovery capabilities.

5.4 The Paradox of the Paradigm's Practitioners

The Adaptive BC approach introduces a significant paradox: It makes it both less and more difficult to prepare the Adaptive BC practitioner for a successful career.

On the one hand, it is less difficult to train an Adaptive BC professional because there are no specific activities that he or she must master in a particular way. He or she does not have to be an expert in a particular standard or best practice, know the ins and outs of the BIA, become proficient in probability calculations for quantitative RAs, or the like. As we have learned, one size does not fit all, and there are innumerable pathways to continuously improve recovery capabilities. Certain BC activities may work well for some organizations but are a waste of time in others. Particular BC tools and techniques will be effective at one point in time but not at another, and both may need to change over time. As long as measured improvement continues, there are no longer any resolutely required steps.

On the other hand, if there is no particular set of practices to master, it makes it more difficult for the BC professional to learn his or her craft. No longer can you provide your organization's newly appointed BC lead with a binder of best practices, Internet templates, and tabletop exercise examples, and then expect success. There is the growing recognition in the BC industry, as there has been recently in project management, that soft skills are indispensable to successful BC planning. If we are actually to become *business* continuity experts, we must become equipped to learn the business of the business. Indeed, the situation is now vastly more complicated because it is no longer enough to learn about BC methodology – the finest practitioners of tomorrow must have a thorough mastery of related disciplines, soft skills, and business operations.

5.4.1 Structuring an Academic Program

This is no small challenge. If we think of a possible set of academic, training, and/or professional certification courses, the curriculum must not only explore the topic of BC, but also a long list of related topics from related fields. To help make this point and guide future instruction, below we provide a potential outline for just such an educational program.

Traditional Business Continuity

- Section One: Know your neighbors.
  - Emergency management, life safety, and physical security.
  - Risk management.
  - Crisis management.
  - Continuity of operations.
  - IT disaster recovery and cyber security.
  - "Resilience" (an interdisciplinary development).
- Section Two: Regulations and related standards.
  - ISO 27001 and NIST SP 800-34.
  - ICS and CERT.
  - Sarbanes-Oxley.
  - Industry-specific regulations in banking/finance, healthcare, and government, e.g., ERISA, FERPA, FFIEC, and HIPAA.
- Section Three: Traditional business continuity best practices.
  - NFPA 1600.
  - BCI Good Practice Guidelines.
  - DRI International professional practices.
  - ISO 22301.
- Section Four: Traditional business continuity techniques.
  - Business impact analysis.
  - Risk assessment.
  - Exercises and audits.
- Section Five: Software tools.
  - (Survey of existing tools; list determined at time of course.)
- Section Six: Case studies (to be supplemented with case studies that are company-internal or more local).
  - Hurricane Katrina, 2005.
  - California Pepperdine wildfires, 2007.
  - Tohoku earthquake and tsunami, 2011.
  - Christchurch earthquakes, 2011 and 2016.
  - Hurricane Sandy, 2012.
  - Australian bushfires, 2015.
  - Malheur National Wildlife Refuge occupation, 2016.

Adaptive Business Continuity

- A critical look at traditional business continuity.
  - The tip of the iceberg.
    - Concerns from practitioners.
    - Concerns from thought leaders.
    - Critiques from academics.
  - Areas needing growth.
    - Need for a more robust methodology.
    - Need for enhanced metrics.
    - Need for emphasis on business value.
    - Need for more rapid evolution.
    - Need for more emphasis on small and medium businesses.
  - Specific problems with specific practices.
    - Obtain explicit executive support.
    - Produce a business impact analysis.
    - Set recovery time targets.
    - Conduct a risk assessment.
    - Document the plan.
    - Test the process.
    - Deliver training and awareness.
- Know your new neighbors.
  - Project management.
    - Traditional.
    - Agile.
    - Project Management 2.0.
  - Continuity process improvement.
    - Lean (and its neighbors, Kaizen and Kanban).
    - The lean entrepreneur.
    - Six Sigma.
- Adaptive business continuity.
  - The proper scope for business continuity.
  - The capability and constraint model of recoverability: constraints.
    - Loss.
    - Restrictions.
    - Together: aperture.
  - The capability and constraint model of recoverability: capabilities.
    - Resources.
    - Procedures.
    - Competencies.

- o Metrics, measures, and calculations.
  - ▪ Preparedness.
  - ▪ Recoverability.
- o Establishing a BC program.
- o Continuously improving capabilities.
- o Exercising.
- o Nonlinear and Gestalt thinking.
- Case studies: (list determined at time of course).
- Putting it all together: Where do we go from here?
  - o Next steps for the industry.
  - o Next steps for you.

Special Topic: Exercises

- What is the point of an exercise?
- Exercise v. test.
- Types of exercises.
  - o Walkthrough.
  - o Tabletop.
  - o Simulation.
  - o Functional.
  - o Multi-functional/full-scale.
- Key objectives of an exercise.
- Key components of an exercise.
- Measurement and metrics.
- Facilitation skills.
- "Postmortems" and lessons learned.
- Tracking and organization.
- Group projects.
  - o Create an exercise.
  - o Facilitate an exercise.
  - o Critique an exercise.

Special Topic: Project Management

- Theory.
  - o Traditional project management.
  - o Agile project management.
  - o Project Management 2.0.
  - o Bringing project management to bear for Adaptive BC.
- Practice.
  - o Project management for BC programs.
  - o Stakeholder engagement and management.

- o Awareness and culture.
- o Tracking, reporting, and forecasting.
- o Potential deliverables.
- Group projects.
  - o Create a plan.
  - o Critique a plan.
  - o Implement a plan.

Special Topic: Capstone Project

- Identify and secure a partnership with an organization.
- Identify the long term and short term BC objectives of the organization.
- Identify the specific BC approach you will use.
- Create a project plan for your capstone project.
- Create and deliver a presentation outlining the organization's objectives and the value you intend to provide during your tenure.
- Partner with the organization to improve recovery capabilities.
- Measure the results of your work.
- Create and provide recommendations to the organization at the end of your tenure.
- Create and provide recommendations to your classmates at the end of the class.

Additional Topics

- Interpersonal skills.
- Introduction to business (the mini-MBA).
- Leadership.
- Public speaking and persuasion.
- Social media.
- Team dynamics.
- The global economy and international cultures.
- …And the like.

The purpose of this educational program outline is not to offer a definitive guide to BC instruction. The point is to provide an idea of the many different types of topics that the Adaptive BC practitioner will need to know and the experience he or she will need to have. The best professionals in our industry, as in any industry, have always mastered a wide range of skillsets from many related fields. This will only become more critical as Adaptive BC practitioners move away from a rote set of activities to a holistic approach to preparedness. In a personal note to the authors in November 2016, Dan Dorman, information technology service continuity manager at Alaska Airlines, explains:

> The point is to accept no sacred cows of BC practice, but re-examine existing structures and practices to understand the objective, apply proper theory, and re-

think the best way to achieve the objective within the context of the organization's structure and needs. By taking this approach, most practices will not be inherently good or bad, but merely a good or bad fit to specific needs…. The adaptive approach may be a bit scary or daunting for the newer practitioner who would likely prefer to have an established recipe to follow. But this is one of the things I like most! It forces BC to grow up and be treated and practiced as the profession it should be – you have to understand the theory behind the practice and learn how to apply it.

5.5 Advice and Appeals to Auditors

There is the very real possibility that you may have to satisfy regulatory and compliance requirements while also adopting an Adaptive BC approach. In Chapter 4 we provided a narrative example of how you might accomplish this mixture using the foundation laid out in Chapter 2 and Chapter 3. But a key component of future success will be in the hands of auditors and regulators of BC programs. As such, we wish to take some time to address them and their role specifically.

Most auditors are not BC experts. They are responsible for auditing a wide variety of programs and processes. In order to audit a BC program, they must rely on some very specific criteria. While organizations can create their own audit controls and measures, this may be difficult and may not satisfy an auditor's requirements depending on the auditor. For the immediate future, the most recognized external industry standard is ISO 22301 which represents an improvement on previous standards, and is focused directly on BC instead of emergency management or information technology (IT) disaster recovery. It follows the "plan, do, check, act" methodology found in many other ISO standards. It talks a great deal about how to set up a BC program within an organization, conduct a BIA, and perform a RA. It spends roughly three pages on "business continuity strategy," before moving on to exercising, auditing, and improving the program. Other concerns aside, this layout obliges auditors to focus on the components and products of the program over and above its value and results.

Section 9.1.2 of ISO 22301 requires that, "The organization shall conduct evaluations of its business continuity procedures and capabilities in order to ensure their continuing suitability, adequacy and effectiveness." ISO 22301 says to accomplish these evaluations through exercising, testing, and internal audits. We have discussed our concerns with exercising and testing in previous chapters. So, what about internal audits?

5.5.1 Focus on Measuring Program Effectiveness

Without a way to measure the *effectiveness* of a BC program, the auditor is forced to measure the *implementation* of the BC program instead. In other words, because there has been no way to determine to what degree a BC program is improving an organization's recoverability, auditors have been constrained to focus on the makeup and products of the program itself. The auditor's criteria for evaluation is therefore made up of yes/no items that are easy to tally by way of documentation, such as the following:

- Is there a document that defines the purpose of the BC program?
- Is there a document that names the parts of the organization to be included in the BC program?
- Did the program perform a BIA?
- Did the program perform a RA?
- Did the program do an exercise?

None of these criteria evaluate whether these activities have been done well! Nor do they evaluate to what degree they have made the organization more recoverable following a disaster. They only determine whether the BC program has been set up and is conducting the activities outlined in ISO 22301. You can imagine scenarios where an organization has set up a BC program in line with ISO 22301 that is, for one reason or another, very ineffectual; you can also image an organization with no formal BC program that is very good at responding to incidents. The structure of the program and its activities are no guarantee of improved recoverability.

We would like to suggest that there is a better way, and one that is fully in line with the spirit of ISO 22301: Measure capabilities. How do you satisfy the "evaluation of business continuity procedures" requirement found in section 9.1.2? Evaluate the resources, procedures, and competencies required for recovery. How do you fulfill the purpose, set out in the very first sentence of ISO 22301, to help "protect against, reduce the likelihood of occurrence, prepare for, respond to, and recover from disruptive incidents when they arise"? Measure preparedness, not program deliverables. Identifying the gap between what is needed and what exists provides a quantitative measure that can be reported to leadership. Meaningful metrics can replace an approximation of program maturity. Gap analysis identifies risks and establishes an actionable roadmap for specific improvements.

If BC is properly defined as the continuous improvement of an organization's recovery capabilities, then those capabilities should be the focus of exercise, testing, and auditing. Just because a BC program does not look like the one described in ISO 22301, or any other standard, that is no reason to judge that it is not effective, and vice versa. Auditors use criteria available to them in order to perform their job and meet compliance requirements. But Adaptive BC now provides an alternative for auditors, and one that does a better job fulfilling the wide-ranging purpose of their role. While it will certainly take time, and may be counter-cultural for a while, we would urge auditors to reframe their thinking about how to meet requirements like section 9.1.2 of ISO 22301 by employing measurements of recovery capabilities. We recognize that auditors will likely have to consider both the program's structure and its effectiveness for the time being, but we hope that the emphasis can begin to shift from the former to the latter in due time.

5.6 Forecasting the Future

There is good news. BC is at the point where it can differentiate itself from other related disciplines, freeing the practitioner from serving too many masters. While traditional BC may continue to operate as it has for years, with its supporting institutions focusing more on disaster management than BC, we believe we are offering an alternative.

There are many similarities between Adaptive BC now and Agile project management (Agile PM) in around the year 2001. At that time, project managers in IT had already been using alternate approaches to traditional project management, but with little cross-practitioner organization, synthesis, or systemization. Their approaches had different names like "rapid application development" and "extreme programming," and were used in different pockets in different parts of the world. In 2001, seventeen developers met in Utah and drafted the *Manifesto for Agile Software Development.* This served as a rallying cry around which software developers and project managers could interact and consolidate a new approach. It took years before the manifesto was written, and many more years before Agile became accepted in the mainstream. But now, experts anticipate that several Agile principles will be incorporated into the 2017 edition of PMI's *Project Management Body of Knowledge* (PMBOK), the "bible" for traditional project management.

Importantly, it took years before a set of specific practices for Agile PM were proposed, tested, refined, and accepted. This process was not handled by a central institute. Instead, practitioners continued to experiment with their work and share their results with others. In this way, potential practices became *proven* practices. These proven practices continue to emerge, change, and evolve. They will not remain the same in many years to come, as new techniques are tried, rejected, or added to the practitioner's toolbox. The future of Agile PM will be driven by empirical results if it is to continue providing value.

We believe Adaptive BC is in a similar situation. Will Adaptive BC develop and gain acceptance like Agile PM has? Logically speaking, there are only three possible outcomes for the adoption of Adaptive BC in the industry:

- **Renegade:** Adaptive BC may only find purchase within a few pockets of BC practitioners. In this case, practitioners will likely arbitrarily pick the activities from Adaptive BC they like best and discard the rest; this capricious approach often happens within Agile PM as well. In this renegade situation, it is doubtful whether something like an organized Adaptive BC approach would stand the test of time, though it could lie dormant to be reclaimed in the future, either by academics who are seeking to formalize a BC methodology or practitioners who are seeking better ways to provide value. Either way, it would remain a somewhat subversive approach to continuity planning within the industry.
- **Alternate:** Adaptive BC may be widely adopted as an alternative to traditional BC. Many organizations and practitioners will continue to use the traditional BC

approach for a variety of reasons, with habit and regulatory compliance being the most likely drivers. But many others will seize this opportunity to provide new value to their stakeholders and greater benefits to their organizations. We note that the current situation at time of writing would also allow a new or existing organization to differentiate itself by fully promoting Adaptive BC. Likewise, an institute, center, or academic program could stand out from similar groups by extricating themselves from traditional practices and popularizing Adaptive BC as a genuine alternative.

- **Replacement:** Adaptive BC may replace traditional BC practices. While this is arguably the least likely of the three outcomes, it is not unthinkable. In response to pressure from advances in public policy, academic research, corporate board members, executive management, legislation, "resilience" related disciplines, and a myriad of other drivers, BC thought leaders might be compelled to more carefully define the profession in order to protect it, thereby embracing foundations similar to those provided by Adaptive BC.

A key component of future success will be an increased level of collaboration and sharing between BC professionals. That will be needed for Adaptive BC to take hold. By providing a new paradigm, theoretical models, and a common vocabulary, BC practitioners can more freely share their approaches without fear of exposing confidential information. Developments in technology, pedagogy, and online collaboration will help contribute to this goal. It is not too fantastic to imagine a dedicated conference that brings together thought leaders, practitioners, academics, policy makers, entrepreneurs, and others committed to the advancement of the profession through the active promotion and adoption of an Adaptive BC approach.

As we go forward, new knowledge harvested from numerous disciplines and changes in the global landscape will have impacts we cannot begin to imagine. Assuming we professionals are still needed to continuously improve the recovery capabilities of organizations, we will need to adapt to the times to provide our BC expertise. If Adaptive BC is to gain wide acceptance, it too will need to evolve to meet the needs of the future.

5.7 Closing: Creative Continuity Planning
In closing, it is our belief that continuity planning should be one of the most challenging and engaging careers available. Being a relatively new profession, it avails itself of a mastery that is more possible to achieve than in other professions. There are tremendous opportunities for contribution and advancement. Furthermore, it is a field in which creativity and innovation can be successfully employed each day. Consider the following questions that are representative of typical BC challenges:

- How do we design a dashboard that provides at-a-glance information on recoverability?

- How do we further empower our service owners to act independently and make the best decisions in a post-disaster environment?
- How do we learn what new strategic initiatives the board is planning for the future?
- How do we structure an exercise that will get accounting to show up and engage?
- How would we procure, deliver, and install 15 portable generators if we had only 12 hours to do it?
- How would we protect the specimens in the minus-80-degree freezers if we lost power for more than a day?
- How would we transport and track 264 people if we had to relocate them across town?
- Is there a way to align the purchase of additional resources in support of the organization's new mission statement?
- Sally is the only one who knows how to do X; what if she didn't show up next week?
- What are the most important business drivers for this department and how do they influence our post-disaster response portfolio?
- What if we were forced to stay at work for 48 hours without being able to leave the building?
- What is the best way to apply what we've learned from accounts payable to centralized purchasing?
- Where could we find alternate sources of funding to procure additional resources?
- With whom could we partner to exchange staff members during a disaster?
- Would it be possible to negotiate a reciprocal agreement for the use of office space following a disaster?

Here we are far afield from flood plain maps and N95 masks. We pointed out this paradox above: While Adaptive BC more carefully delineates the discipline, relevant skills have expanded. The competent Adaptive BC practitioner must combine many different abilities to continually improve both the organization and his or her skillsets as well. This need for professional development is not unique to the field of BC, of course – those individuals who become the best in their field most often excel in bringing a number of different skills to bear in their work. Subject matter expertise, problem solving, and critical thinking, along with interpersonal skills and business acumen will all have a role to play in a successful career.

We hope that Adaptive BC can free us for more creative and engaging work in our field. We have spoken with a large number of BC professionals who say in effect, "I'd love to make my organization better prepared for disaster, but I am too busy managing regulatory, compliance, and audit requirements." This is a telling and disturbing statement. Many people recognize the growing divide between actively improving recoverability and satisfying external requirements. The former requires much more creativity and expertise than the latter. But, conceivably, an Adaptive BC approach will provide the kinds of measurable results that will ultimately convince executives and regulators to change their thinking about the accumulation of documents and checklists. Until now, we had little in the way of viable alternatives but now we have an opportunity to stand back and evaluate our vocation.

What will it be like to "dwell" in this Adaptive BC house of ours? It must be a house that we all build together, working to discover and share proven practices. It will take dedication and creativity to build and expand. We will use new metrics to measure twice and cut once. We hope it will be the envy of the neighborhood and attract new residents. And if we do our jobs right, it will help strengthen all our communities for the uncertainties that the future holds for all of us.

"A boundary is not that at which something stops, but that from which something begins." – Martin Heidegger's *Building, Dwelling, Thinking*

References

International Organization for Standardization (ISO). (2012). *ISO 22301:2012 Societal security – Business continuity management systems – Requirements*. Geneva, Switzerland: Author.

Kerzner, H. (2015). *Project management 2.0: Leveraging tools, distributed collaboration, and metrics for project success*. Hoboken, NJ: Wiley.

Kuhn, T. (1962). *The structure of scientific revolutions*. Chicago, IL: University of Chicago Press.

Lean Enterprise Institute, Inc. (n.d.). *What's lean?* Retrieved from https://www.lean.org/WhatsLean/

Appendix A

Measuring What Matters

A.1 Measuring Preparedness

Measuring a department's degree of preparedness is simple in principle: Identify the resources ("R"), procedures ("P"), and competencies ("C") that are needed in comparison to the capabilities that are, in fact, in place. If a department has 75% of the resources, procedures, and competencies needed to recover, then it stands to reason that it is 75% prepared for recovery. Adding together and then averaging the capabilities for a department provides a measure of preparedness that can be mathematically expressed as:

$$\text{Recovery Preparedness} = (R + P + C) / 3$$

Consider a manufacturing example where the company has done some work to prepare, but has no alternate equipment available to it during an extended power outage. For this example, let's say that it has only 20% of the resources it needs, since it does not have another manufacturing site to use, but as much as 90% of the procedures and 90% of the competencies it requires. In this case, we calculate it to be 66.6% prepared, as (20% + 90% + 90%) / 3 = 66.6%. To make these results easier to visualize, we can put them into our preparedness triangle in Figure A-1.

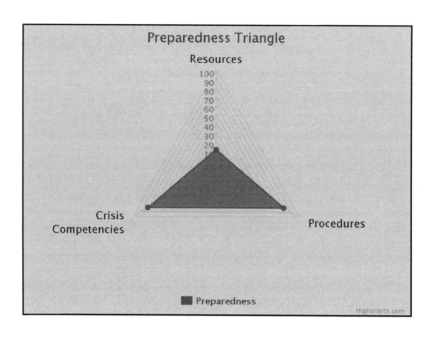

Figure A-1. Manufacturing Preparedness Triangle

Remember that both planning and measurement must take place within the aperture of recovery. This is crucial. The more accurately you can establish both the range of expected loss of people, things, and locations, and the anticipated restrictions of time, cost, and scope, the more accurately you can measure preparedness. As we explained above, preparedness is significantly influenced by the constraints an organization sets for the severity of a disaster it wants to plan for (anticipated loss), and how much latitude it will allow each service during recovery (anticipated restrictions). A department may plan on resuming only 50% of its current functionality given very minimal losses. Another department may need to resume 90% of its full operational capacity even after suffering tremendous losses. How prepared each department is to meet these goals is a feature that can be measured, but must be measured within a set aperture.

Naturally, measurement is going to be easier or harder depending on the complexity of the subject as well as the range and clarity of anticipated constraints. Key considerations include:

- *Complexity*: Measuring an individual service will be easier than an entire organization, and measuring a self-sufficient service will be easier than one with multiple inputs and outputs, etc.
- *Range of loss:* Measuring within a small range will be easier than a wide range.
- *Restrictions:* Measuring for clearly delineated restrictions on time, cost, and scope will be easier than working within vague limitations. For example, "Provide three people to answer email on the 4th floor of 265 Main Street with up to $2,500 in discretionary funds" versus "Restore the help desk."

While measurements may be easier or harder depending on the complexity and clarity involved, they are indeed possible in both theory and practice. The difference will simply be borne out in effort and precision.

A.2 Preparedness Is Not the Same as Recoverability

We are not preparing to prepare; we are preparing to *recover*.

One might be tempted to equate preparedness and recoverability, thinking that if a department is 75% prepared to recover (within the set aperture), they are 75% recoverable. Or, put another way, it seems logical to guess that a department that is 75% prepared to recover has a 75% chance of recovering. Surprisingly, this is not so. Resources, procedures, and competencies are not silos and do not function independently. Each of the three factors *interact* with the other two.

This is best illustrated looking at extreme cases. Suppose a business knows how it will do everything to recover and has the most competent staff imaginable. Imagine it has no additional capital and no resources available immediately prior to a catastrophic fire. Prior to this event, the organization scored a zero percent for resources, 100% for procedures, and 100% for competencies. This averages out to 66.6% preparedness, as $(0\% + 100\% + 100\%) / 3 = 66.6\%$. But, if you were to look at these scores ahead of time, you would rightly assume that they have no chance to recover from a total physical loss.

This means that the measure of preparedness is not the same as the predictor of recoverability.

Let's use a subtler example. Picture a unit that has 75% of the necessary capabilities. The capabilities in this case do not "match up." Some of the procedures reference equipment that makes up part of the 25% of missing resources. These procedures also rely on training and past experience (competencies) that are lacking. Perhaps the majority of resources are ready to go, but employees do not know how to properly deploy or use them (procedures) or the people tasked with execution are terrible at working together in different teams (competencies).

In these examples, what we discover is that, *the factors of resources, procedures, and competencies influence one another.*

So what exactly is the relationship between preparedness and recoverability?

A.3 Calculating Recoverability

There is a relationship between the preparedness capabilities of resources, procedures, and competencies. As an initial proposal, assume that each capability influences the others with equal weight, which can then be expressed as such:

$$\textbf{Recoverability} = \textbf{R x P x C}$$

Let's look at some examples. In the previous case above the business has no offsite resources and no additional capital to purchase such resources. This gives it a resource preparedness of zero percent. Imagine that it has all possible procedures and competencies, giving it measures of 100% and 100%. These scores average out to 66.6% preparedness. Yet it has *no* chance to recover from a total loss disaster without at least *some* of the resources it needs. If you assumed this was the case then your instincts are correct. The recoverability equation confirms that 0% x 100% x 100% = 0%. This predicts a zero percent chance of the business recovering following this extreme example.

Take the example of the manufacturing plant, with 20% of the resources it needs but as much as 90% of the procedures and 90% of the competencies it requires. This gives it a measure of 66.6% preparedness. It seems reasonable to assume that having only 20% of the necessary resources puts it at a great disadvantage. Indeed, 20% x 90% x 90% is only 16%. Perhaps you predicted that a company, similarly prepared, would only be able to recover about one-fifth of its former operations immediately following a disaster. This is borne out in the calculations.

> **Don't Panic About Math:** The math is not meant to be imposing and can be used to a degree of precision that is appropriate to the organization. It would be rather easy to use this model to quickly summarize a unit's level of recovery preparedness: "We estimate the unit has about half of the resources, half of the procedures, and most of the competencies needed to recover 75% of our operations within a week." Yet these equations are robust enough to provide critical measures of preparedness at any level of detail.

The equation *Recoverability = R x P x C* indicates the multiplicative nature of the three capabilities, and that improving (or neglecting) any one factor heavily influences the other two and the organization's recoverability as a whole. This is because available resources, procedures, and competencies might not "match up" to one another. A critical resource needed as the dependency of a procedure may be unavailable. The what, how, and way that a unit needs to recover influence each other. *Each capability of*

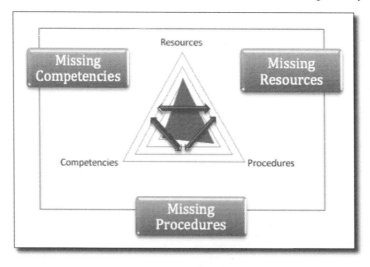

recoverability (R, P, and C) multiplies those factors that are not available at the targeted time of recovery. A simple representation of the interactions might look like Figure A-2.

Figure A-2. Capability Interactions

Table A-1. Interactions of Capabilities

Required Resource	Required Procedure	Required Competency	Outcome
✓	✓	✓	✓
✓	✓	X	X
X	✓	✓	X
✓	X	✓	X
✓	X	X	X
X	✓	X	X
X	X	✓	X

Note that the formula *Recoverability = R x P x C* is a working hypothesis in the truest sense of the term. It should serve as a starting point against which to predict recoverability and measure actual results. Occam's razor suggests that the formula should be kept simple from the beginning, though observed results will likely require developing a more complex formula. Empirical evidence over time will be necessary before a proper and more accurate equation can be developed.

Appendix B

The Adaptive BC Manifesto

B.1 Definition
Adaptive Business Continuity (Adaptive BC) is an approach to continuously improve an organization's recovery capabilities, with a focus on the continued delivery of services following an unexpected unavailability of people, locations, and/or resources.

B.2 Drivers
Despite tremendous revolutions in technology, organizational practice, and global business in the last fifteen years, traditional business continuity (BC) methodology has become entrenched. It has made only small, incremental adjustments, focusing increasingly on compliance and regulations over improvements to organizational readiness. This has led to a progressively untenable state of ineffectual practice, executive disinterest, and an inability to demonstrate the value of continuity programs and practitioners.

B.3 Purpose
Adaptive BC transforms or eliminates the majority of traditional activities in the continuity planning industry. It focuses the discipline and its practitioners on proven practices and away from outdated and ineffectual "best" practices. Adaptive BC better equips continuity practitioners by enhancing their ability to limit potential damage to an organization's brand, capital, functions, and revenue following an incident or disaster.

B.4 Scope
While the principles of Adaptive BC may have implications for information technology disaster recovery, emergency management, life safety, and related fields, they are targeted for the discipline of BC. Drawing from the definition, the scope of Adaptive BC:
- Differentiates Adaptive BC from resilience, sustainability, and other related initiatives.
- Establishes boundaries and guidance for discipline, practice, and critique.
- Provides a framework for ongoing involvement with boards and executives.
- Allows for immediate, innovative, and valuable improvements.

B.5 Principles

There are nine principles in the Adaptive BC Manifesto. No single principle takes precedence over any other, nor is there an expected sequence; together the principles should be applied as holistically as possible. They appear below in alphabetical order.

B.5.1 Deliver Continuous Value

Practitioners should not wait to deliver value all at once, at the conclusion of their preparedness efforts (even if this were possible). Instead, work should build upon itself so that practitioners are continually providing deliverables that are useful to the organization. Adaptive BC adopts relevant practices of agile, lean process improvement, and other proven practices to enable continuous incremental value.

Practitioners should create deliverables that can stand alone in manageable chunks. Practitioners should segment work into business relevant outcomes, producing frequent, shorter-term, additive, customer-informed deliverables that provide value early and often.

Strict methodology and predetermined deliverables should not dictate the creation and delivery of value. Deliverables must be informed both by the direct needs of individual executives and department leaders within an existing situation, culture, and mission, and also by the expertise of the practitioner.

Adaptive BC discourages a sequential approach. Continuous value, coupled with the core mission of continuous improvements in response and recovery capabilities, leads to the adoption of a nonlinear approach that adjusts to ongoing feedback from all participants. The order in which the practitioner delivers value should be dictated by the situation, not the methodology.

B.5.2 Document Only for Mnemonics

The goal of Adaptive BC is the continuous improvement of recovery capabilities, not the accumulation of documents.

Evidence clearly demonstrates that most people cannot pick up an unfamiliar and complicated plan at time of disaster and use it for an effective and efficient response. Documentation alone must not be the primary guide, desired deliverable, or measure of preparedness efforts.

Documentation serves only to support thinking and discussion involved in preparedness. Each responder must have as much of a visceral, immediate, and intuitive understanding of the roles, responsibilities, and actions required of him or her as possible.

Documentation is effective only inasmuch as it provides a reminder of the processes that participants developed and practiced over time.

B.5.3 Engage at Many Levels Within the Organization

Traditional planning methodology focuses on gaining executive support. This exclusivity of focus follows from the fallacy that the majority of necessary information, resources, and support for a successful continuity program are known and controlled by executives.

Many individuals from many levels of the organization greatly influence preparedness outcomes. The continuous improvement of recovery capabilities requires identifying and gaining the support and ongoing engagement of these key individuals and not just executives.

The practitioner must obtain meaningful information in order to effectively prepare the organization for disaster. Most times such information can only be obtained from front line staff or subject matter experts, and often only after having first built a relationship of trust.

Furthermore, it is not the practitioner or the executives who will be restoring systems and services at time of disaster. Response and recovery will require dedicated effort from people at every level of the organization. These are the people who most need to know the procedures and possess the competencies to continue the organization's services. Developing these capabilities requires appropriate and ongoing engagement.

B.5.4 Exercise for Improvement, Not for Testing

Traditional continuity standards call for measurements but are unable to offer examples. As Brian A. Jackson of the Rand Corporation notes, "The limits of many of the means of assessing preparedness have led to interest in the use of exercises…. As a result, whether or not a plan has been exercised is frequently used as a proxy measure for assessing its preparedness value" (Jackson, 2008, p. 9).

BC tests are not reliable measures of recoverability. There are significant limitations in using a test to simulate a real disaster, and serious problems exist in using such an exercise to validate an organization's ability to hit its defined recovery point objectives (RPOs) and recovery time objectives (RTOs).

Exercises should be used to support the continuous improvement of recovery capabilities. They should neither be used as tests or verifications of recoverability nor as reviews of planning documentation. As such, the focus of exercises should be to:

- Get comfortable working and making decisions in a (simulated) post-incident or post-disaster environment.
- Know the structure and practice the initial actions of designated response teams.
- Increase awareness of both existing and missing resources, procedures, and competencies needed to respond and recover.
- Identify areas and owners for short- and long-term improvements.

B.5.5 Learn the Business

Traditional continuity planning focuses practitioners more on methodology and prescribed compliance than on the genuine effectiveness of the work performed. Practitioners often do not understand the business and are unable to address the real concerns of executive leadership.

Adaptive BC encourages practitioners to learn the mission and culture of each department, and to understand the systems and services involved. Response and recovery processes cannot just be bolted onto a department's pre-existing structure and environment. Alien and artificial processes are not easily adopted and are likely forgotten or discarded at time of disaster. Processes that align with the day-to-day nature of the department will be more effective when most needed.

Practitioners must move beyond merely collecting data about the business, and instead improve their business acumen by learning the vision, mission, and operations of each area within the organization as well as the language of leadership within the context of continuity of services.

B.5.6 Measure and Benchmark

Measurement is crucial to Adaptive BC. Traditional continuity planning relies on the accumulation of deliverables or conformity to defined standards as metrics. This oversight results in an inability to demonstrate the business value of practitioners' efforts to executives and other key stakeholders.

The final measure of preparedness is the effective response and actual recoverability of a system or service (or a holistic collection of both) at time of disaster. Organizations cannot afford to wait until time of disaster to know to what degree they are prepared to recover from a significant physical or staffing loss.

Measuring an organization's capability to respond to and recover from an unexpected unavailability is straightforward. Measurement should focus on the following three factors:

- Resources – the degree to which resources that will be required at time of disaster will be available.
- Procedures – the degree to which each individual responder fully knows and has internalized his or her duties at time of disaster.
- Crisis competencies – the degree to which each individual responder, operating in conjunction with other responders, will be able to function effectively throughout the duration of the disaster.

See additional research on this topic at www.readinessanalytics.com

Measurements indicate where an organization can invest to improve its capabilities to recover. Benchmarking demonstrates that such investments have provided the intended results. Practitioners must benchmark existing levels of preparedness as early as possible within an organization, and then again at regular intervals.

Measurement and benchmarking provide a quantitative foundation for Adaptive BC. In this way the organization can be confident that the defined processes, additional resources, and improved competencies are contributing to the desired result – continuous recoverability improvement.

B.5.7 Obtain Incremental Direction from Leadership

Traditional continuity methodology insisted that the practitioner obtain formal support from executive leadership before any work could begin. Standards dictated that all program objectives be identified, documented, and approved by the executive team before the practitioner could even begin work to prepare the organization.

Adaptive BC believes that executive leaders know their business well enough to identify the most critical functions and put the right people in charge of them, thus providing a command and control structure for the preparedness program and its practitioners. Work can begin quickly within individual areas based on the specific needs and knowledge of the accountable and assigned leader in each area.

Using an incremental approach, the practitioner can consistently deliver value and make beneficial course corrections based on regular feedback. The successful practitioner of Adaptive BC must carefully navigate competing constraints while ensuring that board members and senior leaders are aware of their risks for fiduciary accountability, loss of revenues and capital, inadequate or inapplicable insurance, and impact to brand. Practitioners should partner with individual leaders to determine the appropriate actions and investments that will improve the organization's capability to respond to and recover from disaster, while keeping such efforts aligned in the context of business priorities.

B.5.8 Omit the Risk Assessment and Business Impact Analysis

The risk assessment (RA) and the business impact analysis (BIA) form the backbone of traditional continuity planning. They are considered fundamental components in virtually every best practice guide and industry standard. Employing these two practices leads practitioners along a trajectory that further entangles their work in the many related techniques of traditional continuity planning, along with the negative outcomes of these techniques. Practitioners should eliminate the use of the RA and BIA.

B.5.8.1 Risk Assessment

The results of the RA may lead the practitioner, leadership, participants, and organization as a whole to prepare for and mitigate threats that never materialize while other unidentified threats materialize instead. Preparing for the wrong threats is a waste of resources and may lead to a false sense of security that further jeopardizes the organization.

Some threats, such as cyberattacks, disgruntled employees, and utility or infrastructure disruptions, are identified and mitigated but materialize nonetheless. It is precisely because bad things will happen, despite the best efforts of very capable risk managers to prevent them, that continuity planning is so critical.

There are also significant liabilities for continuity practitioners who do not possess the training and expertise to properly implement and follow through on the RA. Risk assessment is a technique of risk management, a discipline with its own body of knowledge apart from BC. Administering a proper RA and implementing the resulting action items may necessitate deep knowledge of actuarial tables, information security, insurance and fraud, state and federal regulations, seismological and meteorological data, and the law. Typical continuity practitioners do not possess such deep knowledge; those who do are most likely specifically trained as risk managers. Adaptive BC practitioners as such should eliminate the RA from their scope of responsibility.

B.5.8.2 Business Impact Analysis

The purpose of a formal BIA is to identify an organization's services along with the potential daily or hourly loss, usually in terms of money, that a disruption of the service would have on the organization. Over time, the purpose of a BIA has changed, expanded, and become indistinct. The term *BIA* now often includes recovery time objective (RTO) and recovery point objective (RPO) data, response and recovery strategies, upstream and downstream dependencies, and other information.

The BIA as a measure of estimated losses should be abandoned. Its main purpose was to help leadership identify the most critical services and to set a prioritization for continuity planning efforts. The discipline should eliminate the BIA because:

- The goal of quantifying the impact of disaster is likely a nonstarter from the beginning. Numerous commentators have identified numerous deep flaws at the core of the BIA practice. Rainer Hübert's definitive paper, "Why the Business Impact Analysis Does Not Work," makes a compelling argument for the industry to abandon the practice of BIA work entirely because of the "very costly and even fatal misinterpretations and misrepresentations" inherent in the process (Hübert, 2012, p. 36).

- Executive leadership can be trusted to identify critical services based on their experience and knowledge of the organization and therefore can set general direction and prioritization for preparedness planning.

- The proper sequence to restore services at time of disaster will depend on the exact nature of the post-disaster situation, a situation that cannot be predicted ahead of time. Because the organization must be flexible and responsive to the situation as it unfolds in real time, recovery time targets and a prescriptive recovery sequence should not be predetermined.

Due to the increasingly nebulous and confused understanding of the term *BIA*, along with the many connotations and associations that the term has within traditional continuity planning, both the practice and term itself should be entirely abandoned in Adaptive BC.

B.5.9 Prepare for Effects, Not Causes
Adaptive BC focuses on the three major effects of an incident:

1. Unavailability of location.
2. Unavailability of people.
3. Unavailability of resources (physical or virtual).

> **A Note About Locations:** Locations are the physical environments in which people perform their work using the things they need. They are reserved for space that people and things must occupy in order to support a given service. An argument could be made that *location* belongs to the category of things. But we find it helps to think of locations as a separate category. Where *things* define an item of specific makeup and performance, *locations* can vary so long as they provide the space and environmental requirements (water, power, security, temperature, etc.) for the people and things to operate effectively.

A vast number of circumstances and combinations of cascading events can lead to one or all of these effects. An organization cannot responsibly afford to plan for so many causes. Fortunately, a robust response and recovery strategy can be generated and effectively executed from a short list of intelligently combined options.

The organization can mix and scale a portfolio of response and recovery processes as the incident unfolds and the situation changes. Often the response to effects can be relatively simple if the staff are trained to evaluate from among a short set of known options and then act as practiced in advance. This allows the organization to remain flexible and efficient in its management of the incident.

> **Note:** The manifesto was originally made available to the public on September 15, 2015 under the name "Continuity 2.0 Manifesto," then updated with "Adaptive Business Continuity" nomenclature on October 19, 2016.

B.6 Postscript
We should expect Adaptive BC to evolve.

This is neither a principle nor a corollary derived from the nine principles, though it should not be surprising given the nature of the Adaptive BC methodology and its focus on flexible and incremental approaches to produce continual value.

Adaptive BC should remain open for critique and improvement, serving as an ongoing proven practice, with hopes that an orderly, structured, and systematic approach can be established to support it.

B.7 Corollary: Adaptive BC Is Not Resilience

While commentators and academics will deduce many corollaries from the original nine principals of Adaptive BC, this one is of such particular import that it should be called out from the start:

Adaptive BC is not "resilience."

Resilience is an inter-discipline. Resilience does not represent a discipline in its own right; rather it connects theoretical and practical tools from a set of disciplines in a unique way and therefore warrants its own sphere of study, practice, writing, funding, and subject matter experts.

Organizational and community resilience is in an uncertain state at present. There is significant debate as to which disciplines resilience should pull from and how to measure its effectiveness. Continuity planning is one discipline among many that will likely contribute to the inter-discipline of resilience. But business continuity should no more morph into resilience than should information technology disaster recovery, cyber security, risk management, sustainability, or strategic planning.

Table B-1. Adaptive BC Manifesto Summary Matrix

Deliver continuous value.	Practitioners dictate the work according to sequential methodology and provide documentation at the end of long cycles.	Customers direct the work according to needs and culture; practitioners provide frequent, shorter-term, customer-informed deliverables.
Document only for mnemonics.	Practitioners create documents as final and required deliverables.	Customers create documents as mnemonics.
Engage at many levels within the organization.	N/A. (Practitioners focus buy-in efforts exclusively on executives.)	Practitioners consciously engage many people at many levels of the organization.
Exercise for improvement, not for testing.	Auditors conduct exercises as a test of the ability to recover within RTO targets.	Departments participate in exercises to practice and improve response and recovery capabilities.
Learn the business.	Practitioners collect data about the business.	Practitioners strive to understand the culture and operations of individual organizational areas.
Measure and benchmark.	Practitioners count the numbers of documents, exercises, and refresh dates.	Practitioners and customers measure preparedness and recoverability.
Obtain incremental direction from leadership.	All executives approve the complete scope of the program before launch.	Individual executives provide iterative direction.
Omit the risk assessment and business impact analysis.	Practitioners require completion of RA and BIA documents before planning can begin.	N/A.
Prepare for effects, not causes.	Experts focus externally – identifying and preparing for a host of specific threats.	Departments focus internally – improving response and recovery capabilities for the unavailability of locations, people, and resources.

References

Hübert, R. (2012). Why the business impact analysis does not work. *The Business Continuity and Resiliency Journal, 1*(2), 31-39.

Jackson, B. (2008). *The problem of measuring emergency preparedness: The need for assessing "response reliability" as part of Homeland Security planning.* Retrieved from http://www.rand.org/content/dam/rand/pubs/occasional_papers/2008/RAND_OP234.pdf

Credits

Kristen Noakes-Fry, ABCI, is Executive Editor at Rothstein Publishing. Previously, she was a Research Director, Information Security and Risk Group, for Gartner, Inc.; Associate Editor at Datapro (McGraw-Hill), where she was responsible for *Datapro Reports on Information Security*; and Associate Professor of English at Atlantic Cape College in New Jersey. She holds an M.A. from New York University and a B.A. from Russell Sage College.

Cover Design & Graphics:	Sheila Kwiatek, Flower Grafix
eBook Design & Processing:	Donna Luther, Metadata Prime
Copy Editing:	Nancy M. Warner
Publishing & Marketing Intern:	Sarah Patton

Philip Jan Rothstein, FBCI, is President of Rothstein Associates Inc., a management consultancy he founded in 1984 as a pioneer in the disciplines of Business Continuity and Disaster Recovery. He is also the Executive Publisher of Rothstein Publishing.

Glyn Davies is Chief Marketing Officer of Rothstein Associates Inc. He has held this position since 2013. Glyn has previously held executive level positions in Sales, Marketing and Editorial at several multinational publishing companies and currently resides in San Francisco, CA.

Rothstein Publishing is your premier source of books and learning materials about Business Resilience, including Crisis Management, Business Continuity, Disaster Recovery, Emergency Management, Security, and Risk Management. Our industry-leading authors provide current, actionable knowledge, solutions, and tools you can put in practice immediately. Rothstein Publishing remains true to the decades-long commitment of Rothstein Associates, which is to prepare you and your organization to protect, preserve, and recover what is most important: your people, facilities, assets, and reputation.

About the Authors

David Lindstedt has more than 15 years of experience in project management, higher education, and business continuity. He has taught courses for Norwich University, The Ohio State University, and Tulane University. He is the founder of Readiness Analytics, a company that offers The Readiness Test™, Household Continuity assessment, and an Adaptive Business Continuity tool. Dr. Lindstedt also serves as the Director of Program Management with the Office of Distance Education and eLearning at The Ohio State University, inspiring innovative instruction through emerging technologies. From 2005 to 2012, he directed Ohio State's Enterprise Continuity Management Program, partnering with over 200 units to protect services such as centralized  purchasing, childcare centers, information technology, steam generation, and even a hotel.

David earned his Bachelor of Arts degree in philosophy, with minors in psychology and political science, from Valparaiso University and received his MA and PhD degrees in philosophy from Tulane University in New Orleans. He is a Certified Business Continuity Professional (CBCP) with DRI International and a Certified Project Management Professional (PMP) with Project Management International. David serves on the Editorial Board and is a frequent contributor to the *Journal of Business Continuity & Emergency Planning*. Dr. Lindstedt has published in international journals and presented at numerous international conferences.

Mark Armour is currently the Director of Global Business Continuity for Brink's Inc., a worldwide secure logistics provider, where he leads the company's Business Continuity, Disaster Recovery and Crisis Management Programs. He has nearly 15 years of experience in the business continuity profession, much of that time spent leading programs and efforts for Fortune 500 companies. He has also managed the corporate response effort to dozens of events, including Hurricanes Katrina and Ike, Superstorm Sandy, wildfires in California and Canada, as well as numerous floods throughout the continental US.

Mark is a Certified Business Continuity Professional (CBCP) through DRI International. He is also President of the North Texas Chapter of the Association of Contingency Planners and a member of BC Management's International Benchmarking Advisory Board. Mark has been published in the *Journal of Business Continuity & Emergency Planning* and presented at numerous international conferences.

NEW!
4th Edition of Andrew Hiles' International Classic

The Closest You Can Get to a "Body of Knowledge" for Business Continuity – All-in-One Comprehensive Book from an Acclaimed Founder of the Profession

"Andrew Hiles was the main driver in the formation of The Business Continuity Institute. His teachings have provided great leadership to our profession... If you only read one Business Continuity book this year, make sure this is it."

– Lyndon Bird, Technical Director, The Business Continuity Institute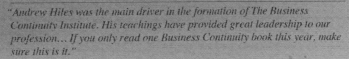

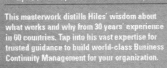

This masterwork distills Hiles' wisdom about what works and why from 30 years' experience in 60 countries. Tap into his vast expertise for trusted guidance to build world-class Business Continuity Management for your organization.

This 4th Edition is the most international, comprehensive, readable exposition on the subject available. It now includes:

- New, extensive chapter on supply chain risk – including valuable advice on contracting.

- New or enhanced sections: * horizon scanning of new risks * multilateral continuity planning * BCP exercising/testing * professional certification * impact of new IT/Internet technologies

- Extensive, up-to-the-minute coverage of global/country-specific standards, with detailed appendices on ISO 22301/22313 and NFPA 1600.

- Chapter learning objectives, revealing case studies and vivid examples, self-examination and discussion questions, forms, checklists, charts and graphs, glossary, index.

- 500-page book + hundreds of pages of downloadable resources, including project plans, risk analysis forms, BIA spreadsheets, BC plan formats, exercise/test material and checklists.

- Instructional Materials – including syllabi, test bank, slides – for use by faculty in college courses and professional development training will be available in late 2014.

"The most comprehensive coverage of all the aspects of developing, implementing, and maintaining a BCM system... a full global perspective on BCM today."

– Michael Howbrook, Director of Education, Telfort Business Institute, Shanghai, China

Andrew Hiles, Hon FBCI, EIoSCM, is an internationally renowned practitioner, consultant, and trainer of two generations of Business Continuity professionals. He is founding director, First Fellow, and Honorary Fellow of the Business Continuity Institute. In 2004, he was inducted into the Business Continuity Hall of Fame by CPM Magazine for demonstrating consistent high standards over time and global reach. He has authored, edited, or contributed to 15 books and has written over 250 published articles on business continuity topics for leading international magazines. Hiles' dedication to training new generations of BC leaders is evidenced by his being among the first to provide truly international training in enterprise risk management, business continuity, and IT availability management in some 60 countries, as well as successfully pioneer BC training in Africa, the Middle East, China, Pakistan, and India.

"In both English-speaking and non-English-speaking countries, Andrew Hiles' training courses and publications are in great demand. This 4th Edition is the most comprehensive book available... will guide students and business continuity management practitioners and be read by corporate and political leaders and policy-makers worldwide."

– Dr. Adil S. Mufti, Vice Chairman, ICIL-Pakistan

Business Continuity Management

Global Best Practices
4th EDITION

by Andrew Hiles
Hon FBCI, EIoSCM

Kristen Noakes-Fry, Editor

CONTENTS

DOWNLOADABLE RESOURCES, including
editable project plans,sample BC plans,
BIA spreadsheets, checklists.

©2014 , 520 pages + Downloadable Resources
ISBN 978-1-931332-35-4, paperback 8.5x11
ISBN 978-1-931332-76-7, ebook

ROTHSTEIN PUBLISHING
A Division of Rothstein Associates Inc.

Rothstein Publishing: your premier source of books and
learning materials about Business Resilience – including
Business Continuity, Disaster Recovery, and Risk, Crisis,
and Emergency Management. Our industry-leading authors
provide current, actionable knowledge, solutions, and tools
you can put into practice immediately.

www.rothsteinpublishing.com
info@rothstein.com

203.740.7400

🐦 twitter.com/RothsteinPub   📘 facebook.com/RothsteinPublishing   in linkedin.com/company/rothstein-associates-inc.

New eBooks
From The Rothstein Publishing eBook Collection

Adaptive Business Continuity: A New Approach
David Lindstedt, Ph.D., PMP, CBCP and and Mark Armour, CBCP
Kristen Noakes-Fry, ABCI, Editor
(A Rothstein Publishing Collection eBook) June 2017
ISBN: 978-1-944480-4-0 (EPUB)
ISBN: 978-1-944480-41-7 (PDF)
172 pages

The preparedness planning industry is at a turning point. Circumstances demand that professionals look at business continuity (BC) and its practice in new ways. Adaptive Business Continuity: A New Approach offers an alternative to make your BC program more effective. Adaptive Business Continuity will improve your organization's recovery capabilities.

The Manager's Guide to Simple, Stategic, Service-Oriented Business Continuity
Rachelle Loyear, MBCP, AFBCI, CISM, PMP Kristen Noakes-Fry, ABCI, Editor
(A Rothstein Publishing Collection eBook) May 2017
ISBN: 978-1-944480-38-7 (EPUB)
ISBN: 978-1-944480-39-4 (PDF)
145 pages

You have the knowledge and skill to create a workable Business Continuity Management (BCM) program –but too often, your projects are stalled while you attempt to get the right information from the right person. Rachelle Loyear takes you through the practical steps to get your program back on track.

The Manager's Guide to Risk Assessment: Getting It Right
Douglas M. Henderson, FSA, CBCP Kristen Noakes-Fry, ABCI, Editor
(A Rothstein Publishing Collection eBook) March 2017
ISBN: 978-1-944480-38-7 (EPUB)
ISBN: 978-1-944480-39-4 (PDF)
114 pages

Risk assessment is required for just about all business plans or decisions. As a responsible manager, you need to consider threats to your organization's resilience. But to determine probability and impact – and reduce your risk – can be a daunting task. Guided by Henderson's The Manager's Guide to Risk Assessment: Getting It Right, you will confidently follow a clearly explained, step-by-step process to conduct a risk assessment.

ROTHSTEIN PUBLISHING
A Division of Rothstein Associates Inc.
Brookfield, Connecticut USA
www.rothstein.com

www.facebook.com/RothsteinPublishing

www.linkedin.com/company/rothsteinpublishing

www.twitter.com/rothsteinpub

I

New eBooks
From The Rothstein Publishing eBook Collection

The Manager's Guide to Cybersecurity Law: Essentials for Today's Business
Teri Schreider, SSCP, SISM, C | CISO, ITIL Foundation Kristen Noakes-Fry, ABCI, Editor
(A Rothstein Publishing Collection eBook) February 2017
ISBN: 978-1-944480-30-1 (EPUB)
ISBN: 978-1-944480-31-8 (PDF)
168 pages

In today's litigious business world, cyber-related matters could land you in court. As a computer security professional, you are protecting your data, but are you protecting your company? While you know industry standards and regulations, you may not be a legal expert, but fortunately, in a few hours of reading rather than months of classroom study you could be.

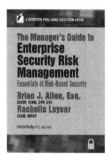

The Manager's Guide to Enterprise Security Risk Management: Essentials of Risk-Based Security
Brian J. Allen, Esq., CISSP, CISM, CPP, CFE
Rachelle Loyear MBCP, AFBCI, CISM, PMP Kristen Noakes-Fry, ABCI, Editor
(A Rothstein Publishing Collection eBook) November 2016
ISBN: 978-1-944480-24-0 (EPUB)
ISBN: 978-1-944480-25-7 (PDF)

Is security management changing so fast that you can't keep up? Perhaps it seems like those traditional "best practices" in security no longer work? One answer might be that you need better best practices!

The Manager's Guide to Business Continuity Exercises: Testing Your Plan
Jim Burtles, KLT, MMLT, Hon FBCI Kristen Noakes-Fry, ABCI, Editor
(A Rothstein Publishing Collection eBook) November 2016
ISBN: 978-1-944480-32-5 (EPUB)
ISBN: 978-1-944480-33-2 (PDF)
100 pages

Your challenge is to maintain a good and effective plan in the face of changing circumstances and limited budgets. If your situation is like that in most companies, you really cannot depend on the results of last year's test or exercise of the plan.

ROTHSTEIN PUBLISHING
A Division of Rothstein Associates Inc.
Brookfield, Connecticut USA
www.rothstein.com

f www.facebook.com/RothsteinPublishing

in www.linkedin.com/company/rothsteinpublishing

y www.twitter.com/rothsteinpub

II

New eBooks

From The Rothstein Publishing eBook Collection

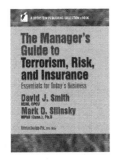

The Manager's Guide to Terrorism, Risk, & Insurance: Essentials for Today's Business
David J. Smith, MSM, CPCU Mark D. Silinsky, MPhol (Oxon.), Ph.D
Kristen Noakes-Fry, ABCI, Editor
(A Rothstein Publishing Collection eBook) October 2016
ISBN: 978-1-944480-26-4 (EPUB)
ISBN: 978-1-944480-27-1 (PDF)
120 pages

As a manager, you're aware of terrorist acts, are considering the risks, but sense that you need more background. How might terrorism occur?

The Manager's Guide to Handling the Media in a Crisis: Saying & Doing the Right Thing When It Matters Most
James E. Lukaszewski, ABC, Fellow IABC, Fellow PRSA, BEPS Emeritus
Kristen Noakes-Fry, ABCI, Editor
(A Rothstein Publishing Collection eBook) September 2016
ISBN: 978-1-944480-28-8 (EPUB)
ISBN: 978-1-944480-29-5 (PDF)
120 pages

Attracting media attention is surprisingly easy – you just want it to be the right kind! If an event causes the phone to ring and TV cameras to appear in your lobby, you need confidence that the people who happen to be at your worksite that day are prepared.

The Manager's Guide to Quick Crisis Response: Effective Action in an Emergency
Bruce T. Blythe Kristen Noakes-Fry, ABCI, Editor
(A Rothstein Publishing Collection eBook) August 2016
ISBN: 978-1-944480-23-3 (EPUB)
ISBN: 978-1-944480-22-6 (PDF)
117 pages

Avoid being "blindsided" by an unexpected emergency or crisis in the workplace – violence, natural disaster, or worse!

ROTHSTEIN PUBLISHING
A Division of Rothstein Associates Inc.
Brookfield, Connecticut USA
www.rothstein.com

f   www.facebook.com/RothsteinPublishing

in   www.linkedin.com/company/rothsteinpublishing

www.twitter.com/rothsteinpub

III

New eBooks
From The Rothstein Publishing eBook Collection

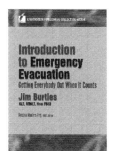

Introduction to Emergency Evacuation: Getting Everybody Out When It Counts
Bruce T. Blythe Kristen Noakes-Fry, ABCI, Editor
(A Rothstein Publishing Collection eBook) July 2016 ISBN: 978-1-944480-14-1 (EPUB)
ISBN: 978-1-944480-15-8 (PDF)
120 pages

When it's not just a drill, you need to get it right the first time. If an emergency alert sounds, are you ready to take charge and get everyone out of the office, theater, classroom, or store safely?

The Manager's Guide to Bullies in the Workplace: Coping with Emotional Terrorists
Vali Hawkins Mitchell, Ph.D, LMHC, REAT, CEAP Kristen Noakes-Fry, ABCI, Editor
(A Rothstein Publishing Collection eBook) July 2016
ISBN: 978-1-944480-12-7 (EPUB)
ISBN: 978-1-944480-13-4 (PDF)
120 pages

As a manager, you can usually handle disruptive employees. But sometimes, their emotional states foster workplace tension, even making them a danger to others.

Creating & Maintaining Resilient Supply Chains
Andrew Hiles, Hon FBCI, EIoSCM Kristen Noakes-Fry, ABCI, Editor
(A Rothstein Publishing Collection eBook) July 2016
ISBN: 978-1-944480-07-3 (EPUB)
ISBN: 978-1-944480-08-0 (PDF)
120 pages

Will your supply chain survive the twists and turns of the global economy? Can it deliver mission-critical supplies and services in the face of disaster or other business interruption?

ROTHSTEIN PUBLISHING
A Division of Rothstein Associates Inc.
Brookfield, Connecticut USA
www.rothstein.com

www.facebook.com/RothsteinPublishing

www.linkedin.com/company/rothsteinpublishing

www.twitter.com/rothsteinpub

IV

Made in the USA
Columbia, SC
22 December 2017